INFLUENCE

Women Inspiring Change

AN AUTOBIOGRAPHY BY:
GERRY VISCA

Their story is your story

INFLUENCE

Women Inspiring Change

Published by Redchair Branding Inc.
Hamilton, ON, Canada
www.gerryvisca.com
Copyright © 2017 by Redchair Branding Inc.

All rights reserved.
ISBN: 978-0-9939129-3-1

Written by Gerry Visca. First Edition
Art Direction by Redchair Branding Inc.
Editing/Proofreading by Natalie Wanner & Angela Kontgen
Printed and bound in Canada

For Angela, my love, my light and my lifesaver!

For the 11 Influencers that believe in the energy of everyday

people doing extraordinary things.

CONTENTS

My story is your story

AUTHOR'S NOTE

#whyguy Gerry Visca

*A*s I reflect on the past ten years of my life the people that I have surrounded myself with humble me. Every person has served as a brilliant teacher. Each one of these angels was put onto my path at the perfect moment. My job was simply to listen with the intent to understand the bigger picture of my life and more importantly, my role in the universe.

It was in 2007 when I finally decided to take 100% responsibility for my life and the one I desired to create. I jokingly share in my talks that I didn't know what the hell I was doing but I always knew *Why.* As I became more passionate about building up people, rather than buildings, I decided to leave the field of architecture in 1999, after investing a decade in that profession.

I loved presenting and creating, so I went on to found a hybrid marketing and branding company called: *Redchair Branding.* We captured several international branding awards and it was this journey that kick-started the inspirational work I live today.

Leading up to 2007, I was ready for the greatest reinvention of my life. Everything changed the moment I decided to change the way I was looking at life. I live by the mantra: *When the student is ready, the teachers appear.*

Jack Canfield served as one of the greatest influences in my life. Upon spending a year immersed in his *Success Principles*, I eventually attracted the opportunity to share the stage with him in 2008. Following that pivotal event, I began carving out the time to ignite my deeper passion and purpose, which was to inspire everyday people and their ideas to action.

The next eight years of my life went by in a blink. Isn't that how life seems to pass? Just a brief moment in time. Before you know it, you and I will find ourselves floating within a cosmic stew of universal information and consciousness. However, before we transition into the next chapter of our spiritual existence we have an opportunity to inspire eleven thousand influencers in the world. With the state of our world today, it is everyday people, no longer waiting for someday or someone else, but rather stepping into their bigger inspired influence that will change the trajectory of our precious world. This is the greater intention of this book. If each of us stepped into our influence and inspired eleven people to do the same this would create an awesome ripple effect in our world. I've always seen it and I will continue to hold this in my heart.

So Why this book?

I conceived the *Influence project* three years ago. That's what's so cool about the energy of 'seeding great ideas'. As you begin living in an inspired state, ignited with deeper levels of passion and purpose inspired thoughts enter your cerebellum and you are simply compelled to take action. Up to this point I had written and published around eleven self-help books, audio programs and a series of inspired publications. However the energy of the *Influence Project* always fascinated me. As I was stepping into my own Influence, I began to live and breathe the following questions:

What creates and ignites a person's influence?

Why do we follow others?

How does their inspired energy live on and influence our world?

I decided at the time that I wasn't quite ready to write and publish this book so I parked it deep into the attic of my mind, knowing full well, that when the time was right it would resurface in an explosive way. Life just seems to unfold this way and I love learning to let go and trust in the flow of it all.

In 2016 I decided to write and publish, what I call an 'un-self-help' book and audio CD titled: *I Don't Know What the Hell I'm Doing!*® This was a thrilling ride! It became an inspired journal-like book. Like all of my inspirational projects it aligns with my mission of inspiring *1 Million Why's* in the world. The intention of this book is to help one dig in and do the work on arriving at the answers to big questions around one's deeper driving Why. Let's face it, in such a busy world, we usually do a half-assed job at answering the big questions of our life. We are always seeking something and someone outside of ourselves for the answers. So I called it an 'un-self-help' book because I truly believe that we were born knowing the answers and all we really need to do is live the questions and do the work. This book was intended to help one also blow away all of the crap we build up around ourselves keeping us from truly seeing the bigger picture of our lives. Only then can you truly fixate on the end prize; your deeper, driving Why.

So with all this inspired Why work I became known as the *Why Guy*. What I know for sure is that what lights up my heart and soul is being on this journey to help people answer the only question that truly matters: **Why am I here?**

In this busy, disconnected world, it's become a very challenging question for people to answer. I listened to my life partner when she shared with me years ago that it was my gift to help people see their deeper Why when they were unable to.

The energy of: *I Don't Know What the Hell I'm Doing*® combined with my sixteen year-old daughter being diagnosed with *Stage 3 cancer (Hodgkin's Lymphoma)*, in July of 2016, sparked a new way of writing for me. For the past twelve months I had been ferociously gobbling up autobiographies of influencers that I admire: Film makers like *JJ Abrams* and *George Lucas*; *Defyeneurs* (inspired entrepreneurs) like *Steve Jobs, Issy Sharp, Howard Schulz* and *Richard Bramson* ignited my fire further.

Women Inspiring Change

I love inspiring movies about our human and spiritual journeys, especially ones where the meanings and messages are not always self-evident, where you have to really reflect and go back to it again. I believe life's learnings often unfold this way.

Around the same time, my inspired mentor *Jack Canfield* published my story in his newest book titled: *Living the Success Principles*. That was a true honour and it moved me to tears to have my story captured. I decided it was time to construct a new architecture for writing. My 14th book project was titled: *Big Dreamers*. It features eight autobiographies of everyday people that were dreaming big. I believe the world has stopped dreaming. We have fallen into line and conformity without much resistance. Society has conditioned the dreamer right out of us and no wonder so many wake up around their mid-thirties depleted, numbed out and wondering "Is this all there is?"

We have evolved into a society where we have chosen convenience over the blissful challenge of going after our dreams. We suppress our true passion for our soul and lean our ladders along *disenchanted walls*. If we are aware of a dream inside of us, we often park it for someday when the kids are older or the mortgage is paid off. Here is the thing, *someday is an illusion*. The truth is life is brilliant and brief.

The energy of my book *Big Dreamers* ignited a new way of capturing the deeper essence of people. I find that stories have a meaningful way of bringing to the surface powerful insights and inspiring messages. The outcome of this energy ignited this new book *Influence.* It was time to plant the seed that I conceived years ago.

So Why These Influencers?

I chose to publish women inspiring change. I was raised by a single mother with a spirit of a lion. I have coached hundreds of women and I am inspired by the strength of their spiritual awakening and gifts they bestow onto humanity. I spent many hours personally interviewing each of the featured *Influencers.* Each question was intended to extract the inspired insights that unveil the richness of their *influence.*

Over the past two years I have had the privilege of getting to know their soul's purpose. Each one of them touched my heart in the previous publications. I believe in each one of them. They are here for a reason and they are becoming more and more clear on their deeper, driving Why. Through this state of being, these influencers are inspiring others around them to embrace and step into their own influence. That is the true essence of influence; *an energy that emanates outward from an inspired state and ignites it in another.*

These stories have touched my heart and ignited my soul. This is no ordinary book; it's sole purpose is to inspire the *influencer* that

Women Inspiring Change

lives and breathes deep inside of you. When you choose to step into your influence, you will summon a new and powerful force that surrounds you. The inconsequential will soon fade away enabling you to focus on living through your unique gifts.

I want to thank each one of the featured *influencers* for the gift of being a part of their inspired journey. I hope you reach out to them and allow their energy and influence to wash over you like a beautiful waterfall.

Help us create a world of 11,000 Influencers:

As you become inspired, share the energy and help us create a wonderful ripple effect in our world. Consider ordering *two copies*, one for you and one to gift to someone and inspire the influence in them. Or even more amazing, make a list of eleven people you know and you wish to gift the book to or simply let them know about it. We call this a new *ROI* for the world, where we all *Reach Out and Inspire* others. Imagine the inspired conversations and energy this will create in your own world and the impact it will begin to have.

This is the world I have imagined and each day I am inspired to leap out of bed and create. This is a world of inspired *influence.*

Gerry Visca #whyguy

Inspirational Speaker | Author | Publisher

"**THE WORLD NEEDS YOUR INFLUENCE. CREATE WHAT YOU WANT MOST IN LIFE.**"

~ Gerry Visca

The Top Reasons Why the World Needs Your Influence.

1. The world's energy shifts when we step into our Influence.
2. We are born with a unique purpose that is meant to elevate others.
3. The World is Helped by You when you get under the Influence of your deeper **WHY**.
4. Your belief inspires us all to take action.
5. The world continues to live in fear and scarcity when we shrink from our Influence.
6. Your Influence is your Legacy.
7. Future generations will be served as we model what it is, to truly Influence.
8. We are at a time when the world needs everyday Influencers.
9. The world has forgotten its way.
10. The world needs you to remember why you are here.

The Top Beliefs That Hold Most People Back

1. It is selfish to shine a light on our greatness.

2. "Who am I to change and influence the world around me?"

3. Influence is about position and power.

4. I have to attain a certain status and success before I can influence.

5. I don't have time to Influence.

6. There is so much negativity in the world.

7. I am defined by what I do and what I have.

8. I am alone in the world.

9. I need to have it all figured out before I step in.

10. Just give me the 3 easy steps to success.

1. Tosca Reno

The Influence of Getting Real

"I exist to influence." ~ Tosca Reno

*T*osca Reno's mother and father witnessed the horrors of the *Second World War*. They immigrated to Quebec from occupied Holland in 1957, with nothing but an unborn child. She shared with me the deep sorrow of the rejection she faced from her mother even from inside her womb.

Unfortunately Tosca's mother was filled with a deep sense of *malevolence* towards her unborn child throughout her pregnancy. *Tosca, the beloved (not a term of endearment)* was eleven months older than her *'Irish Twin'* sister, who arrived in the cold snowy city of Quebec, shortly after immigrating from a war-stricken Holland. As her father faced the trauma of war, her mother struggled to *dig* herself out of the cold depression and six feet of snow...that surrounded her life.

An emotional Tosca shared with me how hard she worked for her mother's love... from a tender age. The unending pursuit for perfection and motherly affection became the catalyst for an arduous life of pleasing others. *"I found myself always having to be more for...others, more beautiful, harder working, smarter and better behaved...just to keep the peace at home,"* she sadly recounted.

~ **Inspired Insights** ~

INFLUENCERS IGNITE THEIR INNER BEING

You are born into this world as a beautiful, untouched being of light and pure perfection.
This inner being is always inside of you, regardless of what others say.

From the age of six, Tosca continually excelled in school. Her teachers planned to advance her from Grade one to three as a result of her superior performance. She found herself disinterested in school... the traits of a genius in the making. While her classmates struggled with a course load of six subjects, she excelled and advanced with ten. She did whatever she could to *out perform* others. This was her way of *rising above* the challenges of her home life.

Tosca experienced the incessant pressure to over achieve and fulfill abusive obligations in her home life. Her mother invested an inordinate amount of time teaching her how to read and write from a very early age, the future passions of Tosca's life.

She grew to love writing as a result of her long-held desire for her mother's affection. She excelled at writing and received awards and recognition throughout school. *"The anguish of my parent's perilous journey echoed throughout our home. I never felt beautiful or that I was enough. The only way out of this emotional war that raged inside of me was through achievement. Words and writing ignited my personal power. It allowed me to dream a new reality."*

She carried with her years of guilt and distress for the *demeaning* energy bestowed onto her and her younger sister. *"The need for perfection followed me throughout my whole life. I developed a beauty complex, which is ironic since I chose a career in the fitness industry."*

Playing sports like soccer nurtured her spirit and *kick-started* a feeling of control in her life. She was a quiet and diligent student so this sport gave her the space to unleash her pent-up rage. *"I adored my soccer coach; Mr. Woodill. I was the highest goal scorer and continually won MVP. I learned that physicality made my body and spirit roar,"* she recounted.

~ Inspired Insights ~
INFLUENCERS NURTURE THEMSELVES

In this fast-paced world, you must nurture and condition your mind, body and spirit on a continual basis. Seek out healthy outlets like: physical exercise and meditation as harmonious ways to balance your energy.

The years of driving herself towards being smarter, better and stronger created a *disconnect* between perception and reality. *"I conditioned myself by dimming the light so others around me wouldn't feel dark and small,"* she tearfully shared.

Tosca persevered through her teens as a result of *blind faith.* She believed in her talents and experienced greater levels of joy when she lived through her gifts. Her instruments for writing served as her sword, slashing through the demons of doubt and disbelief. She was praised for her writing and unanimously voted by her high school classmates as *Valedictorian.*

"I always felt like a nerd and an ugly duckling in high school, never knowing where to fit in," she recounted. Little did she know at

Women Inspiring Change

that time, being recognized by her peers ushered in a new era for finding her voice. She now found a way to broadcast her words from a high school stage.

Her pairing of the written word with the confidence of her voice elevated her inner belief. *"I couldn't get enough of it. Through out the years, I restlessly searched for a global microphone to broadcast my passion and purpose."*

Towards the end of high school, she craved studying literature and becoming a celebrated author. Her grades were the top of the class and she wanted to attend *Queen's University in Kingston, Ontario* under a full scholarship referred to as: *The Tri-Colour Awards*.

Unfortunately, she was at odds once again, with her parents who impressed their desire for her to pursue a career in medicine. *"I hated the sight of blood. For too long, I witnessed my father going through numerous epileptic seizures and heart attacks. Becoming a doctor was the furthest thing from my mind."*

A sharpened scalpel wasn't the tool she dreamed of holding. Visions of a microphone and a light-filled stage with a captivated audience filled her soul. She didn't need to know the *how*; she believed her passion would light the *way* for an inspiring future.

She struggled and fought her way through university. She suppressed her deeper passions that lit up her soul. She succumbed to the pressures of pleasing her parents. *"I hated how I felt in university...studying science. It wasn't me and I felt like I lost myself during those years."*

~ Inspired Insights ~

INFLUENCERS IGNITE THEIR WHY POWER

The World is Helped by You (WHY) when you are living your passion and purpose.
When your inside voice bellows louder than the external noise, you've mastered your life.

In her earlier years, she felt vilified for standing out. *"I learned to take the hits by living as a quiet warrior and a survivor. I became aware of my ingenious super power to think, write and creatively share my story...as a way to push through the pain."*

She can see clearly now that her exceptional gifts, mental and physical strengths were bestowed on to her by her parents. She always possessed an unprecedented and resilient strength. At fourteen, her *unyielding* strength emerged the day she singlehandedly propelled her family car from a snow bank, so her parents wouldn't be late for the airport.

~ Inspired Insights ~

INFLUENCERS ACTIVATE THEIR SUPER POWER

Inside each one of us resides a super power that we've been given at the time of our birth.
These unique abilities are experienced when we ignite and live through them.

Tosca had a long-held desire to *drive* her intellectual gifts of writing her words, and sharing her story. Shortly after graduating from university, she got married and became pregnant and once again...parked her dreams.

She worked at various jobs in pharmaceutical sales and eventually gave birth to another two children. *"I knew my choices were limited at this point. Providing for my children... became my priority."*

She found herself attracted to her first husband as a result of not doing the inner work on herself. *"He was an abusive replacement for my mother. He even pushed me down the stairs as a result of becoming pregnant with our first daughter. I never felt I had a choice so I endured the relationship for seventeen years,"* she added.

Despite this incredulous seventeen year journey with over ten moves, she overflows with gratitude for the sheer strength that her first husband taught her. *"This strenuous time in my life taught me resilience and that I could overcome any challenge."*

Leading up to her 39th year she began conceiving a plan to finally leave her first husband. At 204 pounds, the heaviest she had ever been, she found herself feeling hopeless and depressed. *"I saw no vision for myself but I knew if I was going to leave my husband and support my children, I would not be a drain on society,"* she recounted.

She proceeded to lay the foundation for her future independence. She knew she was intelligent so she returned to school to become a teacher and proudly earned a Bachelor of Education at the age of forty.

~ Inspired Insights ~
INFLUENCERS BELIEVE THEY ARE WORTHY

The moment you believe you are worthy and take powerful action, you create the conditions to receive the love you deserve. All spiritual growth comes from within.

Upon leaving her first husband, she eventually landed a teaching position in *Georgetown, Ontario.* Glimpses of light slowly cracked their way into her new life. She patiently worked her way back to wellness. *"I didn't know what I was doing but I had an intention of getting fit. It just so happens, when the student is ready the teacher appears."*

While teaching at a *Georgetown* school, she found herself drawn to a beautiful little girl name Chelsea, who was traumatised from her mother's recent death. Chelsea's protective father Robert dropped her off every morning and over time he and Tosca nurtured a deeper relationship.

One day she revealed her keen interest of interior decorating that enticed Robert to invite her to redecorate his custom home. Little did she know that this man would become a significant influence, later on in her life and that his home would be hers.

As their friendship grew, Tosca shared her passion for fitness. *"In a state of disbelief, he dared me to accept his challenge of training me to become a body builder. I felt I had nothing to lose so I accepted his challenge."*

After twelve months of rigorous training, the discipline of which she devoured greedily, she went on to compete and place in her first body building competition in *Las Vegas, Nevada. "He often commented, that my mental strength was even greater than my physical."*

Her training in body building, far exceeded the muscular physique she was creating. He influenced her to believe in her inner strength and that she could surpass any temporary pain. The dramatic physical changes she experienced suddenly attracted *Oxygen Magazine* to publish her transformation. *"This is where I found my true voice to share my story."*

It was as if the vision she had experienced on stage during her *Valedictorian* speech, suddenly burst to life. Robert witnessed the incremental growth of her passionate followers who hungered for more of her experience. It didn't take long for him to envision a bigger world and a massive following for Tosca. *"Even though I didn't know where to begin, he encouraged me to write a book. So in 2006, during a six hour flight to Victoria, BC I sat and wrote my first book, The Eat-Clean Diet®."*

The book was published in January of 2007 where it quickly sold out its first 5,000 copies in two short weeks, making it an instant best seller in Canada. *The Eat-Clean Diet®* went onto become a *New York Times* best-selling book and book series that attracted a massive following.

"I felt I was hitting the mark by being authentic and sharing my new found vitality for life. I was empowering readers to step into their brilliance. I wanted women to experience what I felt, stepping out from the shadows and into the light."

She knew what it felt like to be overweight, hopeless and floundering with no purpose. She had lived with the thought of ending her life. She perceived herself as a candle and an insightful light for others wishing to transform their lives. *"It gave me tremendous excitement and I just wanted to keep doing it. It wasn't about being famous. It was about touching people that felt broken...*

like I did for so many years. I longed to walk with them as they experienced a transformational journey," she recounted.

In order for Tosca to truly stand in her power, she needed to *shift* herself by learning how to nurture her mind and body. She learned to develop a new level of discipline in her physical training. She mastered the skills of time management as a result of extensive travelling, writing and growing family obligations.

"My shift was synonymous to that of a butterfly's metamorphosis. I had to shed my skin. I needed to rewire my conventional thinking. I incorporated new ways of eating and nourishing my body."

In her past, she was terrified of standing in the light. With her newfound success as a best-selling author, she had to embrace an unfamiliar public image. *"I was worried that people would discover the 'real me' and think I was a...fake,"* she openly shared.

~ Inspired Insights ~
INFLUENCERS BUILD NEW SUCCESS HABITS

The common denominator amongst all successful people stems from their willingness to replace past conditioned habits with new powerful ones.

Today, she longs for a harmonious alignment of her heart, mind and soul. During her years of physical and transformational changes, she feels she missed out on nurturing a deeper *spiritual* connection. She is seeking an unconditional love for herself and the

Women Inspiring Change

purpose that she lives through. She craves *soulful* connections with herself and with others.

She articulates her relationship to Robert that lasted from 2002 to his passing in 2012, as a *delirious* roller coaster ride. *"It was deliciously wild,"* she said. *"I was distracted by fame and material goods. In the midst of the bright lights...I missed out on feeding my soul."*

Her *delirium* came crashing down in 2011 when Robert's son Braden died at the young age of twenty-four. Two decades earlier, he suffered extensive brain damage as a result of being struck by a car. *"Even though his passing was a gift to eliminate his suffering, his death...devastated us all. Braden's years of perseverance inspired me to challenge my physical body and push beyond the pain. When I ran my first triathlon and competed in a marathon...I ran for him,"* she tearfully shared.

Braden's immobility influenced Tosca to experience every physical movement as a gift. When she trained rigorously in the gym, she did not perceive it as punishment.

The year 2011 was an arduous one for Tosca and Robert. Within a year of his son's death, Robert now found himself battling terminal cancer. Tosca had to endure yet another fatal twist to her life.

She shares the emotional passing of her love, Robert, in April of 2012 and how he was *spiritually surrounded* by his loving family. *"I wanted him to die in the serenity of his home. All of us helped him cross over to the other side. My heart ached with his passing. He was the love of my life."* She came to perceive cancer as a ruthless teacher that takes but also teaches.

Little did she know that the man she called her *life partner*, left a destructive loop that twirled her spirit in the most profound ways. Tosca didn't have much time to grieve. She was propelled into taking over his publishing business. *"Gerry...you wrote a book called, I Don't Know What the Hell I'm Doing®...well I didn't know what the fuck I was doing! I started off looking under the hood of how his business ran and that's where the nightmare began."*

Astonishingly, the accountants revealed that Robert's business had been insolvent for the past five years, prior to his passing. They informed her that she'd have to declare official bankruptcy. *"That was a new kind of horror that began as a result of uncovering the mysteries of his life and a myriad of 'secret keepers' embedded in his business. Unfortunately I was perceived as the last man standing who brought down destruction onto his failing business,"* she shared.

To her bewildered ignorance, she never received the millions of dollars in book royalties that Robert funnelled to keeping his sinking publishing business afloat.

"I felt betrayed, blindsided and destroyed throughout this structure of reality. Over the next twelve months of legal challenges, my daughters and I were suddenly faced with no income and forced to go dark. In my business going dark means death."

Drawing on the energy of the past, she did the only thing she knew how to do, kick into survival mode. During this time of immeasurable healing, she authentically shared how she stumbled to

Women Inspiring Change

discipline her mind, body and spirit. She struggled to displace the hurt and sheer disappointment with the man she loved so deeply.

Her heart had grown cold and dark. The anger of betrayal raged inside of her like a high speed train out of control. She faltered and didn't know who to trust. She pulled her *warrior daughters* in close surrounding her with their strength and light. *"I chose to adopt Robert's daughter Chelsea. When I asked her if she wanted this, she immediately broke into tears and revealed it was her long-held desire."*

~ Inspired Insights ~
INFLUENCERS PUSH BEYOND THE PAIN

When faced with life's many loops, you push through the pain by riding the rails and facing the sinking feeling head on.

A glimpse of hope appeared in the distance as if God suddenly cracked-opened the universe. Her yoga teacher and friend, Angelika, persistently reached out to her. *"Her idea was to teach me how to reconnect with my emotional self through meditation and energy work."*

Tosca eventually picked herself up and sat in on a meditation class. *"At first I didn't trust in the reality she encouraged me to embrace. I was outraged at the notion that Robert and Braden's death was an illusion and that I had chosen these things. I hated being there. Everyone around me appeared so connected and evolved while I felt alone and filled with hatred."*

With no financial stability, she persisted slowly and painfully in rebuilding her business from the ashes. Her daughters helped her where they could. She was forced to sell her book and magazine titles, which she claims, felt like selling her children, just to stay alive. She raised funds by selling her wedding rings and gifts from Robert; cars; furniture and material possessions, just to keep from drowning.

Shortly after, she became entranced with how the *World Health Organization* defined *wellness.* In was in that moment where she began to perceive herself as a fraud. *"Wellness isn't the absence of disease. It's the presence of your nutritional, physical, mental and emotional self. Suddenly, I realized I was only operating on two of those cylinders."*

From that point on she was determined to shift herself into using all wellness gears. She was now prepared to surrender her *white knuckle grip* on the universe and dive deeper with self-love.

The sheer devastation of the past five years became her greatest teacher for embracing a new mental, emotional and spiritual *self.* She intuitively knew, it was time to delve deeper into the uncharted realm of her mind and spirit.

This mental *shift* created a new vibration within her universe and attracted a new set of powerful mentors into her life. *"I knew I couldn't do this alone and I needed help,"* she openly shared.

She defines an *influencer* as being a person whose truth is their passion and whose passion is their purpose. Influencers have an ability to *spark* life inside people. Their energy and light ripples out into the world. *"This energy makes you want to sing, dance and shine. It inspires you to be who you were meant to be in this world,"* she adds.

The road to healing and freedom required a deeper level of *forgiveness* for all of the angels that crossed her path. She began with forgiving her mother for the hardships she inflicted upon her as a child. She expressed gratitude for the gifts and the light that her mother gave her.

"She influenced me to read and write. Through this journey, my mother has grown herself. She still inspires and stands beside me. My first husband gave me my children, my gifts of light. My sister is a courageous heroine and we've been each other's soldiers at war all of our lives. Robert taught me to love, take risks and stand in my power. He showed me the way out of the shadows and into the light," she lovingly shared.

Today, she is surrounded by new influencers. *"Gerry,"* she begins. *"You and your life partner, Angela Kontgen have helped me see the need and the ability to trust again. This is an excruciating and difficult thing for me. Since I met my yoga teacher Angelika in 2004, she has lovingly persevered in bringing me back to the light."*

~ Inspired Insights ~
INFLUENCERS SURROUND THEMSELVES WITH POSITIVE PEOPLE

Surround yourself with people who see your light during the times when you can't see it for yourself.

As we near the completion of our time together, Tosca shared the astounding breakthrough she recently underwent at a *Shaman* healing retreat along with twenty-five other souls. During her *Shamanic Journey*, she unravelled a deep realization to the group, *"I revealed my hidden and ugly secret,"* she tearfully said. *"I've wrestled with an identification of beauty my whole personal and professional life. Deep inside, I've always felt ugly. As I sat their disentangled in my raw and mucus-filled state, the group suddenly surrounded me and broke out into song and celebration. I finally experienced the energy of being aligned with my true self."*

Every generation will hear the echo of Tosca's *influence*. The majestic sounds of people reclaiming their power by nurturing their body temple, will chime in the winds. Her energy will inspire others to emerge from the shadows of disease and darkness and into the light of wellness.

The outcome will be a world that celebrates the best version of us. Her wish for her fellow brothers and sisters is that we positively contribute our unique gifts for the benefit of all humanity.

"The dream and the fuse that I want to strike for my legacy starts within my heart and soul. With God's graces, I will light that fire in the belly of my children. My daughters are my Amazonian warriors and they inspire and influence me everyday. I see this courage and power trickling into my grand daughter who stands in her warrior stance. My wish for her and her generation is to never dim their light and stand strong in whatever path they are meant to take."

Tosca believes that each one of us has a unique role to play in the brief time we've been given on this earth. She hopes her words and her influence inspires generations to ignite the fire in their bellies and embrace the winds of change.

~ Inspired Insights ~
INFLUENCERS ARE CONNECTORS

We will push the human race forward by becoming aware of our connectedness in this universe. Together, we're better.

With an unshakable force she stepped into her truth. With unbridled levels of passion and purpose she owned her power and light. She embraced her inner knowing with a ferocity that coursed through her veins. She unearthed a deeper and more profound voice.

With eyes wide open and a courageous heart she is thrusting herself into an *Amazonian* persona. With a pen at her fingertips and a microphone by her side, she is poised to bellow out her greatness from the rooftops.

This is the purpose that she has been asked to live.

This is Tosca Reno *getting real.*

"**IT'S NOT WHERE WE ARE, THAT MATTERS, BUT IN WHAT DIRECTION WE ARE MOVING.**"

~ Gerry Visca

2. Maureen (MO) Hagan

A World of MOtion

"I exist to create motion...to move people into the direction of their greatness and be bold enough to take the steps forward."
~ Maureen (MO) Hagan

*A*s far back as high school, Maureen (Mo) Hagan always lived with a desire to shape a career that didn't exist. To know the real Mo, is to *live* her passion for physical movement.

Whenever Mo found herself moving, she was in a state of flow and sheer bliss. Movement didn't have to necessarily be a physical sport. It was an energy that coursed through every cell in her body. When she was moving, the world moved right along with her. This *motion* inspired her spirit at whole new levels. It was her *escape* and her silence from the noisy world, around her.

As early as she can remember, she had an intention of carving out her own career. Her passion for movement inspired a *deeper desire* to create something far greater than simply a sport. It's these kinds of powerful intentions, that somehow transport us into the future...that was certainly the case for Mo.

At a young age, she had a glimpse for a *world of MOtion*. Sometimes, that's all we need...a glimpse. Through inspired action and a relentless belief, she moved herself forward and bridged the gap in realizing her vision.

Throughout puberty, Mo didn't realize that movement was a part of her *DNA*. At the time, it served as her oxygen...her life force. *"I needed to move, to be my happiest and my best self. It was only in that state that I could be Mo,"* she recounted. Movement allowed her to show up in life as the Mo she envisioned in her mind. Movement was imprinted in her cells.

Growing up in the 60's and 70's, she often found herself at odds with her teachers, as a result of having a voice and speaking her mind. *"I had a voice and I wanted to use it. I had a body and I wanted to move it."*

Sitting for long hours at her school desk didn't get her juices flow'n! *"In school, I was continually told to sit still and be quiet like everyone else."* Her teachers forced her to sit still for a full day and that didn't serve Mo and her greater self.

It was in *Physical Education (Phys Ed)* where she found her *true self* and her passion for moving her body. *"It was the first time where I really felt permission to move and do what I did best. I had many Phys Ed teachers, but the one that really influenced me to create my desired life, was Ellie Armstrong,"* she enthusiastically shared.

Three decades later, Mo was inducted into her high school hall of fame. She was blown away when her twin sister presented her with a copy of their old yearbook. To Mo's astonishment, was an inscription next to her picture written three decades earlier as if she was writing to her future self. It simply read: *'My ideal career is anything to do with fitness, where I can travel the world, teach and have a career.'* Little did she know at the time, she was living her intention and creating her own opportunities.

Back in high school, her guidance councillors tried to 'box her into an already established career in *Phys Ed*.' They discouraged her from pursuing something that didn't exist. Lying within the depths of her heart and soul, was a new and profound voice that emerged and stood up to the thousands of *no's* and *naysayers'*.

Regardless of *how* her family, friends, teachers and guidance councillors saw her, her inner being had no interest in fitting into a *mold*. She believed she was meant for *more* than just following what society told her she *should* do. She believed the world needed something different. Even though at the time she was unaware of exactly *how* or *what* the *way* looked like, she knew in her heart what she wanted others to experience.

~ Inspired Insights ~
INFLUENCERS FOLLOW THEIR HEART

The path to greater levels of personal fulfillment appears when we follow our own heart.

We ignite our personal power when we carve our own path.

When we silence the external voices, we can actually hear our inside voice.

Like most young kids, Mo endured following the *status quo*. She did her best at *colouring inside the lines* by acting like the perfect daughter and avoiding too much trouble. Throughout her younger years, she intuitively felt that something was missing. *"There's got to be more to life than sitting quietly in the corner and conforming to the rules of society."*

Women Inspiring Change

Following the rules just didn't sit well! It *stirred* her curiosity and invoked *mixed* feelings. She believed that to live her passion would require stepping out of the traditional norm.

~ Inspired Insights ~
INFLUENCERS IGNITE THEIR INNER FLAME

To live your greatest life requires a relentless belief in your inner fire. Your inspired vision becomes a compass and a lighthouse during the darker times when those around you attempt to douse your flame.

"I didn't want to hurt anyone, I simply knew what fired up my soul and I was determined to challenge what others envisioned for my life," she shared.

Mo knew that to create her desired life required a deeper energy of resilience. These challenges shaped the very person she is today. With a sense of determination and defying spirit, she challenged herself and what others deemed possible.

Upon graduating high school, Mo generated momentum with a Physical Education degree from university. Her passion and vision was firmly rooted in her body, mind and spirit. She fixated on the horizon; a career outside of a typical *Phys Ed* degree. She hunkered down and learned as much about health and fitness as humanly possible. She *softy* followed the rules...but internally she *defied* the system by visualizing the game she desired to create.

Her greatest influencers were her *Phys Ed* teachers. Every encounter inspired her to shape her own career. It was as if they reinforced what she didn't want to do. *"I was inspired by them but I didn't see myself teaching Phys Ed. I wanted to break out of the box. I believed I could become a global teacher of motion,"* she recounted.

The people that influenced her most were the ones that stood up for themselves and challenged the status quo. Musicians like *Cher* and *Madonna* and royal icons like *Lady Diana* stood out amongst the others as a result of their relentless tenacity. *"If Lady Diana could break the rules and Cher could say, 'look out bitches...here I come,' then I knew I could do anything I set my mind to,"* she laughingly shared.

She was inspired with these *rebels of change*...the ones that had a voice. *"They were the ones that created change and defined their industry. I saw myself among them and becoming a role model for others. I thought to myself, 'If they could do that in their industry...then why not me in mine?"*

This energy of following and leading continued to ignite her passion and purpose in defining and leading the fitness industry. She envisioned being the *rock star* bellowing her voice from the stage. Her message would be one of *confident defiance*. The people she attracted enriched a deeper learning.

Like a great artist, Mo learned to sculpt her boldness and cultivate her inner confidence. She incrementally strengthened her personal power by surrounding herself with powerful mentors. They inspired her to follow her *joy* and discard everything else that didn't serve her masterpiece...her dream career.

~ Inspired Insights ~
INFLUENCERS VIEW EVERYONE AS TEACHERS

See everyone that crosses your path as your greatest teachers. When you know who you are, what you want and how you wish to serve the world, others play a role in helping you shape your destiny.

Mo was raised in humble surroundings in the 60's. Growing up as a *fraternal twin* brought her a deeper understanding of her desire for individuality. Even though her mom dressed them the same, she recognized and nurtured their different mindsets.

Since the time of her birth, Mo and her sister shared the same crib and a single bedroom, even throughout high school. They were very different and often it was these differences that kept them from recognizing how close they really were as friends.

Mo and her twin shared everything from birthday parties and toys to school friends and celebrations and even the same prom dress, which caused friction and even competition at times.

It was only until they separated by attending different universities that they truly discovered their deeper love and appreciation for one another. *"Later on in life, I appreciated just how close my sister and I were. The 'twin power' that I resisted when we were younger, became a special gift ...years later. I learned to develop deeper levels of love and respect for her."* This remarkable *twin power* revealed itself as *pseudo labour* when her twin sister was actually giving birth.

It was actually through her connection to her fifteen month younger brother that helped instil confidence, individuality and boldness within her. *"Being a twin taught me that you can walk your own path and create your own story...if you choose to."*

Mo learned to thrive in this contrast. She wasn't interested in following a traditional path filled with white picket fences. She saw herself defining her own way... travelling the world and defying the odds, to create her own identity. Being the first-born instilled a level of inner confidence and belief in her ability to lead others.

Leading up to the time of her mother's death, she shared with Mo a deeper appreciation of the leadership qualities that she sensed in her daughter early on. It served as a validation for Mo. She finally learned how much her mother trusted and looked up to her. *"Even though my twin sister and I are like night and day, being a twin invoked a deeper belief in me that I was never alone in the world,"* she recounted.

~ Inspired Insights ~
INFLUENCERS ARE NEVER ALONE

No one in this world is ever alone. A path to greater fulfillment comes when we reach out and embrace one another's differences and unique characteristics.

Within the first ten years of her fitness career, her leadership skills excelled at *Goodlife Fitness* under the mentorship of founder;

David Patchell-Evan (Patch). She learned to challenge mediocrity, cultivate bigger ideas and find her bold voice. *"Patch gave me permission to stand out, speak up and become my own person."*

Throughout the early years at *Goodlife Fitness*, she often felt like a black sheep grazing among a field of white sheep. *"I quickly learned that black sheep are far more valuable than white sheep...so I told myself to go it,"* she laughingly shared.

To her surprise, she had to fight her way through the *herd* to see her ideas realized and implemented. Within this competitive environment, she nurtured a deeper belief in leadership and learned to stand up for herself.

Mo can see the teachings from every challenge that her journey presented. She learned to trust and believe in herself. Her leadership grew as a result of connecting with her inner voice. *"When I listened to my inner voice playing out in my head; whether positive or negative, I was able to reflect on the teaching in that moment. By listening with the intent to understand...I owned my personal power. It influenced powerful decisions and ultimately shaped my life."*

Years of speaking on stage helped her *own* her inner power. It's her sweet spot, her authentic self and the soft chewy centre that she savours. When she plays full out she experiences greater levels of joy. *"I have learned to convert negative thinking into positive action. I don't beat myself up. I simply look to my inner dialogue as my compass of change."*

Mo learned to master her inner dialogue. Unlike most people who needlessly suffer from the voices in their head, she refused to be a hostage to her thoughts. Her inner dialogue continually steered a course correction. Her *true north* appeared as a result of living with a relentless belief in her leadership and acceptance of her *true* vision.

"People don't care about how much you know until they know how much you care. I trust in my ability to tap into my realness and that helps me share my true authentic self with others."

She intuitively knew at a young age that she would influence the world as an *agent of change*. Even though she didn't know *how* that vision would unfold, she believed in what she wanted to experience and more importantly...*why*.

To her surprise, she recently reconnected with one of her mother's former neighbours that she hadn't seen for forty years. *"Mo, as a young girl you always had a passion for gathering up the kids from the neighbourhood and teaching them physical exercise,"* she recounted. At the tender age of seven, little did she know that her *world of motion* was ignited in her neighbourhood.

The conversation leading up to the final hours of her mom's life validated Mo's decision to lead and create a new path for her inspired *way of being* in life. She would inspire a *world of motion* through fitness but in a unique way...Mo's way.

~ Inspired Insights ~
INFLUENCERS IGNITE THE WAY

Influencers don't obsess with the how's. They allocate their energy towards uncovering the deeper, driving why. Their inner knowing ignites the way.

From a young age, Mo longed to experience a sense of belonging. She was driven with a pursuit of excellence. It fuelled her passion to achieve greatness in all areas of her life. She loved proving to people what was possible even when they said it couldn't be.

This internal drive and determination became her fire. It ignited all of her cylinders and fuelled her *super power*. It's not surprising that people who know her best call her...*Mighty Mo*.

When others labelled her as stubborn, Mo defined her unique ability as: determined and driven. When others told her to hold back, follow the rules and live her life by following a *traditional* path, she threw on her *superhero cape* and soared into a realm of possibilities.

~ Inspired Insights ~
INFLUENCERS LEAD WITH LOVE

All of us have a choice to live with fear or love.
When we choose to love ourselves unconditionally, we ignite our super power.

Years of thriving amongst the stars ignited a powerful desire to shape the perception and credibility of the fitness profession. She imagines a world where fitness and health professionals are in equal standing to one another. It is her wish to influence a healthier world where people choose fitness as a proactive means of improving themselves, physically, mentally, spiritually and emotionally.

She lives with a long-held desire to guide people to that next plateau, helping them cross a new threshold of possibility. She is forging a proactive legacy and shaping humanity's perception of the fitness industry. In collaboration with confident professionals, Mo is inspiring a new generation of thought leaders that will proudly carry the torch high into the future. She feels a dramatic shift in her profession is fast approaching.

~ Inspired Insights ~
INFLUENCERS ARE COLLABORATORS

Influencers harness the power of collaborative thought. They seek out like-minded individuals who share common values for the change they wish to create in the world.

Mo intuitively believes her passion and persistence will continue to drive change in herself and others around her. She longs to forge a profound connection with her *inner being*. *"I know I need to surrender my ego in order to shape this experience of profound change in my industry."*

She is keenly rooted in connecting to deeper levels of *why she exists*. She wants to surpass the energy of *simply doing* and master the *art of being*. A part of her still thrives on global recognition from her peers as a motivator of change. *"Today my energy is fixated more to one of contribution. To live in this new way of being, I recognize that I need to go beyond goal setting and open my heart to inspiring others."*

With greater levels of humility, she lives with an energy of service to others. She has learned how to be more present in the moment by giving herself to others. She allocates greater time in helping people achieve greater results in their lives. She got out her own way by helping others find theirs.

Women Inspiring Change

~ Inspired Insights ~
INFLUENCERS UNCOVER THEIR UNIQUE ABILITIES

Great levels of personal fulfillment doesn't come from 'doing more' but by 'being more'.
Serve others through your unique gifts and your purpose.

To get onto this path of inspiring others, Mo shifted her mindset by becoming increasingly observant to the people and the energies she was attracting into her life. She embraced an insight of what I define as: *Be what you seek.*

New and inspiring mentors, coaches and *influencers* flowed into her path. *"I found myself being attracted to these inspiring energies. Instead of resisting it, I opened my heart fully to receiving the gifts that they bestowed upon me."*

By opening herself up to these *synchronicities* she is now cultivating deeper connections with new influencers. She surrounds herself with a cast of *change agents* and like-minded people. Each connection reveals greater depths of self-awareness for the profound influence she desires to create in the world.

"I've always been attracted to the depth and character of people; the ones that defy the odds to define themselves. Whether it's in a book, a movie or face-to-face, I get inspired by the teachings from mentors that I look up to."

Mo gets inspired when she witnesses authentic people changing themselves in order to influence change in others. Titles and resumes don't float her boat! It's the energetic presence of inspiring people that gets her MOJO going.

~ Inspired Insights ~

INFLUENCERS ARE CONTINUAL LEARNERS

Influencers never stop growing. Their hunger for continual knowledge helps them expand their consciousness. As they continue to evolve, so too does their thirst for learning.

"Angela Kontgen; a meditation coach and creator, recently helped me connect to my deeper self through the art of daily meditation. The awareness of my thoughts shifted my mindset," she said.

Like most people, Mo's mindset was conditioned at an early age to *follow the crowd* and doing what others thought was best for her. Influencers that defined sports like global fitness ambassador; *Helen Vanderburg* impacted Mo's belief that she could be and do anything she set her mind to. *"I followed Helen when she claimed the first world championship gold medal for synchronise swimming. Even though I wasn't a strong swimmer, she inspired me to push beyond the fear and train as a synchronise swimmer in University."*

Early in her fitness career, Mo learned the art of making a plan, taking action and persisting until she reached her goals. In 1990, at her first global fitness conference, she met her mentor Helen and they became instant friends. *"With fond admiration, I watched Helen reach epic milestones in her career. She won countless awards and she inspired me to model her actions and pursue the same types of awards."*

What influenced Mo the most was Helen's ability to connect with the hearts of people in the workshops she delivered. Helen influenced Mo by shaping her internal belief systems that she too could define a thriving industry.

INFLUENCERS CREATE MEANINGFUL OUTCOMES

It's not what you say that people remember but how you say it.
When you strive to connect with people's hearts...you win them for a lifetime.

Even though Mo's mom viewed her as living amongst the *crazy ones* her energy influenced her life. As she reflects deeply on the passing of her mom twenty-four years ago, she appreciates the teachings that shaped her character.

"I'll never forget the day she said to me...are you crazy leaving your dream career to become a fitness instructor?" Or the time she told me I was breaking up the family by going on one of my six month back packing retreats."

Little did Mo know, her desire in defining her own path was nurtured in the dichotomy that existed in her upbringing. Her mother's *faint belief* echoed years later through her mother's caregiver. *"I was astonished when her caregiver revealed that my mom talked about me all the time. Apparently my mom expressed how proud she was of me; that I was living my life boldly. She appreciated how I did it my way and was not swayed by what others said."*

This new found awareness filled Mo up with new levels of gratitude. She has released any latent energy of regret from her arduous upbringing. She can see clearly now, her mom showed up exactly how she was meant to. She was an angel of light intended to inspire Mo to ignite her own path.

~ **Inspired Insights** ~

INFLUENCERS LOOK FOR THE LEARNINGS

The universe sends us nothing but angels. Every person in your path was meant to influence you in a meaningful way. The key is to recognize these powerful learnings, the moment they appear.

Women Inspiring Change

Mo believes the defining characteristics that shapes an influencer is someone that is not afraid to stand up, speak their truth and challenge the status quo. Influencers spark curiosity in all of us by inspiring us to look within ourselves and ignite our own level of greatness. Influencers live their lives by inspiring others to lift themselves up.

She defines an influencer as a difference maker, advancing their industry. They serve others as ambassadors of change for humanity. *"Influencers live with kindness and courage. They are unafraid of being radical in their approach towards inspiring change in the world. They help guide people by showing them a path. People like Michelle Obama stand proudly in the light by finding their own voice and creating their platform of change,"* she added.

The following recommendations summarize the *actions* and *new levels of thinking* Mo embraced along her journey of influence:

- *Be proud of who you are and all you are being in the world.*
- *Set a powerful intention for living your passion and purpose everyday.*

- *Nurture your relationships.*

- *Be a connector of people versus having to be the one with the answers. Ask people; What do you need? Who can you connect them with?*

- *Live your core values.*

- *Discover your own path instead of blindly following others.*

- *Practice authenticity; Who is the real you? What is your super power? How can you be of service to others?*

- *Know yourself. Ignite and share your unique gifts and talents with the world.*

- *Lead yourself with integrity by walking the talk. Be the role model that you wish to see in others.*

- *Exercise your body and mind, daily.*

- *Embrace change as a catalyst for growth. Remain relevant by existing in a continual state of curiosity and perpetual learning.*

- *Share your point of view and continually find your voice.*

- *Listen to others with the intent to understand them.*

- *Develop a sense of curiosity and wonder in others.*

- *Lead with your heart instead of a title.*

- *Reject the naysayers. Change the way you look at rejection. No means 'not now.'*

- *Choose to be a change maker and defy the status quo.*

~ Inspired Insights ~
INFLUENCERS LISTEN

Influencers are profound listeners who strive to understand the hearts of others.

They avoid the temptation to reply.

They guide others by helping them seek out the answers

"Being me and leading with my heart, allows me to contribute to the lives of everyone around me."

I am inspired by Mo's determination and belief in her dream to create deeper levels of awareness for health and wellness in all of humanity. *"My definition of health and wellness has always differed from traditional medicine. Even as a physiotherapist, I prefer to teach people to be proactive by managing their own health and to be response-able for their own rehabilitation."*

With a compelling vision and strong voice, Mo is inspiring a world of *self-care* that will help redefine our declining *healthcare*. *"All of us can experience greater levels of pleasure and reduce suffering by taking a proactive stand with our own personal level of health."*

Mo embraces the next wiser chapter of her life with great anticipation and opportunity. She is redefining herself and becoming the change she wishes to see in the others. *"I know I have a significant role to play in this changing world of Baby Boomers. By opening the curtains and drawing back the shades, I'm helping to define a new way as to how the world perceives 'retirement',"* she shared.

Mo's greatest wish for others is to recognize and honour their powerful and internal gifts. We lead ourselves when we choose to do the inner work to grow our best selves and set powerful intentions on how we wish to show up everyday.

~ Inspired Insights ~
INFLUENCERS HONOUR THEIR GIFTS

All of us are here to serve the world in our own special way.
By honouring our own unique gifts we inspire others around us to be and do the same.

Three decades later, Mo caught up with the intention she set for her future self. She is living *the dream life* she envisioned creating many years ago. She is an influencer of change, helping to create a world of *ease*. She travels the world as a *global fitness ambassador* inspiring new levels of awareness for fitness and health.

Through her determination and strength that shaped her as a young girl, she defied the odds and the naysayers and dream stealers that attempted to box her in. She is living in her sweet spot with a sense of flow and ease. Her influence and belief in her vision has helped shape the fitness industry and profession as a whole.

There was this 'chick' who lived one hundred years ago named *Mighty Mo*. She stood up and trusted in her inner being. She lived boldly with a sense of passion and purpose. She believed in becoming the best version of herself. By taking powerful action everyday, she created momentum and influenced a world of MOtion.

"LIVE AS THOUGH YOUR LIFE DEPENDED ON IT."

~ Gerry Visca

3. Kim Fitzpatrick

Rock Your Life

"I exist to empower others to shine." ~ Kim Fitzpatrick

Kim Fitzpatrick lost her birth mother at eleven months of age. Her father remarried a wonderful woman named Cindy when she was twenty months old. Together, Kim's parents raised a beautiful family of five kids, with Kim being the middle child.

From an early age, Kim at certain points, lived with what felt like a conflicting energy and struggled to find her identity in her younger years. *"I longed to uncover where I fit in and who I truly was."*

This search to *define herself* became a powerful catalyst, later on in her life. Giving birth to her first son, Colby on January 11, 2009 and then to her daughter Tessa, shortly thereafter in July of 2011. The birth of her children and passage into motherhood ignited an *'aha moment'* in Kim's brilliant life.

It was as if giving birth sparked a newfound awareness for her place in the world. She was finally embracing and aware of her gifts and her ability to now further transcend her *life lessons* into raising her two beautiful children. *"It was if I was somehow healing myself. It was as if the birth of my children cracked me open and awakened me to the greatness I always had within."*

She lived with tremendous discomfort as a *people pleaser* throughout her whole life. She worked hard to savour and experience the power of the moment. *"I found myself constantly searching for the next best thing because I was feeling unfulfilled... inside."*

Kim experienced learning challenges early on in school as a result of being an exceptionally vibrant, creative and visual student. *"Some people don't know how to handle creative beings,"* she laughingly shared.

She lived with a *robust energy* that needed to burst to the surface for the world to see. As a child, she was determined to learn how to confidently express herself. This at times was confusing. Listening, hearing and ultimately believing the opinions of others, for example, she was too loud, not good enough or smart enough to attend university.

She was innately aware of her *intelligence*, however, she needed to find a powerful vehicle to drive her belief. Throughout her whole life, she was sensitive to the spiritual connection with her birth mother. She attributes a part of her deep passion to radiate her burning energy as a result of this spiritual kinship.

~ Inspired Insights ~
INFLUENCERS DEFINE THEMSELVES

Focus on extracting the juicy parts that define the real you. Shout out your greatness from the rooftops and inspire others with the luminosity of your gifts.

The idyllic vision of her mom blazed Kim's trail. Her explosive and kind energy guided her to the light. Her spirit helped to extract the greatness that resided deep within. *"I often wondered at times how different my life would be if my mom was physically here with me. I have felt her presence and warmth my whole life. It is a beautiful feeling. It was a helpful energy that kept me growing during the most arduous times,"* she emotionally shared.

Little did she know that the person she was seeking to become was actually her *greater self.*

This explosive energy at times created an unrealistic expectation of others. *"I found myself being disappointed on how certain people showed up in my life. "Until I realized that was my own expectation I was setting on others. Today I coach others by inspiring them to meet people where they are at lessoning personal expectations is a big part of that. I embrace everyone's personal path, passions and desire, and meet them where they are at along their unique journey."*

Kim is able to ascertain the deeper learnings from her earlier challenges. She no longer *reacts* to life. She looks for the light inside of everyone she meets. She is aware of what she doesn't want to experience; fear, judgment, constraint and not feeling good enough.

"Life happens to all of us but it's the way I choose to respond that continues to shape my character, my parenting style and ultimately my life. I help my children experience their light and rise above societies' constrained views. I inspire them to believe they can achieve anything they set their mind to. I want to surround them with a shield of belief in themselves."

Kim is learning to release the energy of judgment, anger and other low vibrations that keep us from realizing our full potential.

~ Inspired Insights ~
INFLUENCERS LIVE WITH GRATITUDE

When we live through an energy of gratitude and empathy for others we eliminate the energy of expectation. See others doing their best from their own state of consciousness.

In her early teens, her heart yearned for *self love*, flow and acceptance. She searched for the magic in the experiences that ignited the sparks in life. She had a long-held desire of creating a synonymous life that flowed with greater ease. She continually probed for the next best thing that would bring her greater levels of personal fulfillment. *"I longed to be 'just me' and release the attachment of what others thought and how they perceived me. I craved to silence the self-judging voices inside my head,"* she recounted.

Today, Kim longs for presence and inner peace. She perceives the mind as an incredible machine that has the ability to *wreak havoc* if we are unaware of the power of our thoughts. She desires love, happiness and contentment in all areas of her life. She unabashedly puts herself out there as she strives to live her desired vision.

She takes 100% responsibility for growing into the person she visualized in her mind...as a young girl. She is writing a new chapter in her life by seeing everyday as a gift and an opportunity to move her vision forward.

Her previous story no longer owns her or controls her life. *"My intention is to inspire others living in victimhood that there is a better way. There is a brighter light on the other side of darkness."*

~ Inspired Insights ~
INFLUENCERS FIXATE ON THE HORIZON

Release the energy of the past. Instead, focus on the direction you intend to head in.
Choose to take 100% responsibility for the life you have the power to create.

Kim invested tremendous life energy in pursuing what she believed to be the next best thing. She was preoccupied in landing the corporate job, getting married and having kids. None of those accomplishments brought her joy in the moment. She was unable to receive her gifts and nurture her relationships as a result of not healing herself.

As a victim, she found herself reacting to life versus creating it. *"There are still times when I find myself falling into this state of victimhood...but I now recognize it and get myself out of it quickly."*

Influencers like the late *Dr. Wayne Dwyer* inspired her to refine her skills by looking deeply into her own mirror. *"I employ his technique of 'volleying the ball back'. Too often we take on other people's shit and it gets in the way of our own clarity."*

She averts getting entangled in a *web of judgment*, comparison and competition with other people's energies. As a result of transcendent healing, she has been able to fill herself up. She volleys with a heart of empathy and deeper levels of compassion for others.

Women Inspiring Change

"If you don't like the reflection or the story you are telling yourself, then you can't expect others to be inspired and influenced by it."

INFLUENCERS ARE NOT DEFINED BY THEIR PAST

Your future is not dictated by your past. Where you currently stand does not impact the steps you intend to take. You possess the power to change the reflection you see.

Kim likes to call herself a *self-help junkie.* She *plays* with self-help giants of the world. She intentionally surrounds herself with visionaries, difference makers, change agents and *influencers* that help shape humanity.

She continually seeks out fresh and thought-provoking vehicles to ignite deeper levels of clarity in her own life. Her visceral transformation over the past twelve months is a result of diligently listening, absorbing and applying the learnings from a myriad of inspiring mentors. *"I strive to align inspired learnings with my mission, my being and my message in the world."*

She fundamentally believes that if you don't know what you want in this world then you are lost. Most people find themselves being defined by their TO DO lists without really experiencing significant change in their lives. *"This was certainly my life previously. I often was getting through many days in a stressed out and robotic way. That is not a way to live."*

One of her greatest shifts was when she chose to complete a full workout program; including the nutrition and mindset work accompanied the workout regime in her and her husband's health and wellness-based business. To her wonderment, this seemingly simple daily habit induced greater levels of self love.

She learned to fuel and nourish her body with the right nutrients to stimulate her endorphins. She was pumped to embed this newfound knowledge she gained into powerful action.

"My husband Jamie was my mirror and an instrumental part of this transformational process. If I'm not being my authentic self, he calls me out and that's so important to my growth. I've had to unlearn years of conditioned behaviour and channel my feisty and loving passion," she laughingly shared.

She approaches everything and everyone from a place of pure love and joy.

Kim's dad was one of her greatest teachers. His prominence in the community helped to teach her that she didn't need a profound title to lead and influence others.

"His wisdom taught me many things, and softly taught all of his children to never judge the way other people show up and love you."

She has learned to accept others for *who they are*...beings of light doing their best from their own state of consciousness. She is a human being experiencing a spiritual existence.

Kim's grandmother Carol (her birth mother's mother) inspired her with the purity of her love, light and kindness. She referred to Kim as her *last baby* and was one of many of the "village" that rallied around during that difficult time, helping to care for her sisters, and support her dad and her dying mom.

She savoured the comfort of her grandmother's *Klondike Bars* and the safety of her loving embrace. She is filled with gratitude towards a village of friends and neighbours that rallied around her and her family when they all lost; a mom, a wife, a daughter, a sister and a shining member of the community.

To this day, old neighbours and elder members of her mother's church still stop her on the streets in her hometown, and share the joy they experienced in knowing her mother and being a part of the "village" of support during that sad and difficult time. *"I believe in the influence of community. This is the power that I am working to create,"* she tearfully shared.

She believes that no one in this world deserves to feel alone. *"When we band together and build others up, we inadvertently change ourselves and strengthen our own lives."*

She is centered on helping others *release* their vulnerability in order to let the light of their greatness, open up their hearts. She believes in the power of collaboration and unified wisdom to inspire a world of greatness.

"Everyone has the power and light to create tremendous things. The great minds that we admire, accomplished greatness by working together. When we start to embrace the seeds of other people's ideas and visions, we can create a connected and passionate universe."

~ Inspired Insights ~
INFLUENCERS ARE BIG DREAMERS

Every great idea originated in someone's mind that was told their idea was impossible to realize. Believe in your ideas. The world needs Big Dreamers.

A core attribute that shapes influencers stems from an unshakable belief in their *imperfect* vision and deeper reason for being. Their daily commitment and persistence in nurturing their gift and message, brings it to life. Through their willingness and desire for continual growth, we experience their genius.

"When others witness an influencer's imperfect perfection, they become inspired with a belief that the world is so much bigger. You influence a person to say yes to a better way of living their life rather than existing in a state of fear and victimhood. You can influence from power and fear or through inspiration, love, acceptance and beauty."

Kim embraced the following *actions* and *thinking* along her transformational journey:

- *Apologizing* to herself, her sisters and then to a lot of...other people.

- *Owning* her story and taking 100% responsibility in creating a new one. She was no longer prepared to allow her *past thinking* to own her. *"My actions started with me experiencing peace with myself, my decisions and my past. I had to embrace the shame and guilt."*

- *Channelling* the emotions of fear into love for the people and the relationships in her life. *"I refused to continue allowing fear to be the driver. I learned how to park it in the back seat of my life."*

- *Taking* action with the most *uncomfortable* areas. She knew that without discomfort, she couldn't experience new levels of growth.

- *Conditioning* her mind, body and spirit on a daily basis by showing up as her *best self* in the world.

- *Transcending* all of her own learnings into her own business and to her family by creatively teaching others.

Kim wants to be remembered by her children for being a strong, bold and compassionate mother. She wants to be perceived as a *leader* that believed in people and in herself. She desires to influence the next generation to have fun and adventurously discover the joy of living and playing a full out life. *"I want my children to embrace their emotions instead of thinking they need to be iron-fisted to be successful. Personal equals universal. Kindness is king."*

Inspired influencers like Kim, live with a balance of kindness, vulnerability and inner strength.

She is most proud of retiring from the corporate world at the young age of thirty six and together with her husband Jamie...creating their *own* way of freedom in their families' lives. She is determined to illuminate people that there is a better way to living the freedom that we all deserve.

Her belief in herself, her family and in her way of being is her oxygen source. Her belief doesn't originate from a place of fear, worry and reaction but from one of love, possibility and inspired action.

"When I put my intention of serving others by helping them become their best selves out into the universe, I receive what I need to be connected with. My faith has to be stronger than my fear."

What she knows for certain is that her belief is stronger than her doubt.

~ Inspired Insights ~
INFLUENCERS BELIEVE IN THEIR VISION

"Whether you think you can or you think you can't, either way you're right."

~ Henry Ford

Your unwavering belief in yourself and in your dream will carry you through the necessary discomfort along your journey.

Kim's wish for others is to stop placing so much pressure on themselves to be perfect. *"I lived this way for a long time. I carried around a facade that everything is perfect when in actual fact, it wasn't even close to what I thought perfection was,"* she recounted.

Influencers find the joy and happiness in what they do. *"If you want to rock your life then go ahead and be happy pursuing that."* Her wish for others is to let go of the outcomes and the expectations from others.

Influencers don't fear going against the grain, standing out and doing something different. This is what differentiates them from the rest of the world. They push beyond the fear and are unafraid of failing forward, standing out or looking foolish. Influencers challenge the status quo and themselves for what is truly possible.

How will you know your true potential if you don't take chances and step out of your comfort zone? *"You have to pursue your life unabashedly without a care of what other people think of you. People's opinions of you are none of your business! The more you can release the energy of other people's impressions, the stronger you'll be."*

She influences people to live their best life by shining in their best emotional, physical and mental state. *"On your deathbed...it doesn't matter what other people thought of you but how you lived your dash."*

An emotional Kim shared how every Thursday she visits her mom's tombstone and kneels and prays at her grave. She uses this special time to *reflect* on her desire to sparkle and shine with the *stars* in our universe.

Kim's feet may be firmly grounded but her heart and soul soars into the heavens as if her mom is pulling her greatness up for the world to bask in her shimmering light. She believes the magic unfolds when your inner belief in your ability to sparkle is more vigorous than anything in your external world.

Her wish is for others to start each day more profoundly than when they found it. Become intentional by choosing to make every conversation, interaction, decision and choice more profound than the day before. Imagine a world we would influence if we all chose to make each person's life better. *"The more you genuinely fill everyone else's bucket, the more healed and fulfilled you feel."*

~ Inspired Insights ~
INFLUENCERS INSPIRE OTHERS

The road to greater levels of personal fulfillment stems from our desire to reach out and inspire others.

The following summarizes Kim's *top actions*:

- Be a researcher in your own life. Be intuitive and continually ask yourself if your habits and actions in all areas of your life are serving you. Are they contributing to your happiness? *"When you research deeper into all of areas of your life and identify what is not making you happy, then you have to do something about it."*

- Be *observant* in your reactions.

- Be *reflective* in your decisions and your choices.

- *Set* Big Harry Audacious Goals (BHAG).

- *Celebrate* daily wins, no matter the size. Developing the capacity to honour your wins along your journey will help you reach your destination.

- *Create* momentum by celebrating the start. Consider tackling your daily actions with a five second rule and just go for it!

- *Take* responsibility and control for getting yourself into action. No one is going to do it for you.

Women Inspiring Change

As we near the end of our extraordinary time together, I asked Kim to contemplate the *outcomes* that future generations would experience as a result of her *influence*. She paused and reflected deeply on a similar question she answered in one of my previous publications.

She profoundly believes we can be the change we are seeking to influence in others. She shares that by inspiring change to improve someone else's life, they will in turn become a better parent. *"By inspiring others, you will help alter their original imprinted path."*

When most people become aware of their greatness they are compelled to make a change in their lives and that change has the power to ripple out to multiple generations. *"You have the ability to change your story and your actions the moment you commit to creating a new path and believing it's possible."*

Kim desires to influence a world of significant change through the impact that parents have on their children and their children's families. *"I'm passionate about paying this energy forward by encouraging others to drop the shame and guilt that is not serving them. Eating an M&M does not mean that you failed your diet plan,"* she laughingly added.

When we collectively help one another by paying this energy forward, we are creating a world of deeper self-awareness. *"The more you instil self love, self-acceptance, belief and joy along your amazing journey, the more you will become aware that life is meant to be lived fully. I hope when someone reads this chapter, they believe that they can always be better."*

Most people live everyday, unaware of the fact that they are even unaware. They don't know that they don't know. Kim is an influencer that is forging a deeper level of awareness of our power to initiate change so we can all shine in this world.

By continually living a life from a beginner's mind, you remain a student of life open to receiving the abundant teachings bestowed upon you. All of us have the ability to access this universal energy. *"When people start to look in the mirror with beautiful eyes and marvel at their inner perfection with joy, love and confidence, that's when you own your power."*

~ Inspired Insights ~
INFLUENCERS SHIFT THEIR MINDS

When you change your focus you shift your attitude.
When you change your attitude you begin to shift your habits.
When you change your habits...you change your life.

I asked Kim to share with me who her greatest influence was in her life. She struggled to identify just one. She walked through most of her life feeling alone and disconnected. She longed to define herself and her way of being.

Every step forward, served her profound transformation. She inspires everyone she meets with a sense of joy and a child-like curiosity. As I reflect on what her starry-eyed mother would say, I can hear whispers from the heavens...*"You my sparkly Kim are your own...greatest influence."*

" " **YOU DON'T NEED TO KNOW WHAT THE HELL YOU'RE DOING...**

...BUT YOU DO NEED TO KNOW WHY! "

~ Gerry Visca

Photography by: Jon Blacker

4. Angela Kontgen

Change Your Mind. Change Your Life.

"I exist to help people really notice and experience their one precious life." ~ *Angela Kontgen*

*A*ngela Kontgen was born into a European family as the oldest of three siblings. She recalls the challenge when her family immigrated from *Europe* to *Ontario* and eventually onto *Quebec*, during her high school years.

She was no stranger to the continual relocation of the family home and in her younger years embraced the journey as an opportunity to create new experiences. The eventual move to *Quebec*, however, posed a series of challenges that would significantly *shape the mind* of this meditation coach and creator.

The move to *Quebec* also meant leaving behind some really great friends to start fresh in a new high school. Her dad was facing the pressures of opening a business in *Quebec*, settling his family and transitioning from a very stable and prestigious corporate position; life as an entrepreneur while tasked with opening a new business in *Quebec*.

The greater challenge for Angela was witnessing the serious depression and change in her mother's state of mind. *"The combination of my dad having to work longer hours in setting up a new business combined with the upheaval of the family began to take it's toll on my mother. I equate this time of my life as going from a colour to a black and white movie. Life was good and rolling along and suddenly these changes showed up."*

The family was impacted with a series of episodic events: The death of Angela's grandfather in *Paris*, the transition to a new city and her father spending long hours away from home. These events caused her mother to fade into a deeper state of depression.

"Although, my grandfather lived overseas he was a huge spirit and influence in my life and I loved him so much. He was the most extraordinary human being I ever knew. He had the special gift of just making me laugh and feel connected simply by being together and walking or sipping a cup of tea. I still feel his energy today," she emotionally shared.

The tender age of thirteen is where Angela began developing her survival skills. Feelings of isolation and vulnerability influenced her to figure life out on her own. *"It felt as if anything that mattered at that point...was gone. I settled into survival mode as I felt the absence of my father, the loss of my grandfather and the fading away of the vibrant and present mother I once knew."*

She pushed through the pain by keeping herself constantly busy in a high functioning 'state of doing'. It was through this coping mechanism that she was able to temporarily displace the realities of her current situation.

Interestingly enough, this constant state of *doing* would catch up with her...years later. She even found herself getting mixed up with the people that did not serve her higher good, shallow and troubled relationships and friends. Yet, even surrounded by this turmoil, she discovered ways to shift her energy through therapeutic activities like running and swimming that she knows today were what shifted and improved her state of mind. Running was like a new form of oxygen and also helped attract positive people into her life.

"I felt a bit like Forrest Gump running from one place to the next. Running certainly helped me develop healthy new friendships and became a very positive outlet." Fitness didn't just fill up her *busy* TO DO list; it fuelled her with a new source of purpose. However, the more miles she clocked the greater the distance created between her and her mother. *"She didn't seem to understand or support my need to run. She thought I was going to eventually hurt myself. I even found myself sneaking out of the house to do my runs and to avoid her negative commentaries,"* she recounted.

~ Inspired Insights ~
INFLUENCERS CREATE MOTION

It's not where you currently are that matters but the direction you plan on heading in.
Influencers take 100% responsibility for creating the desired outcomes in life.
They move themselves forward and generate incredible momentum.

Whether it was running from town to town or developing new friendships in school, Angela had a desire to propel her life forward. It was through a constant state of motion that she felt in control of her inner power, quite literally for the first time. *"Because I had no understanding, at this young age, of my mother's state of mind, I developed a desire to not be like her. I had a drive to be different and* not become a person who chose to remain in a state of fear, negativity and doubt and who could not move her life forward."

In her later teens, Angela found herself constantly on the go with a desire to create a life of independence. Upon graduating high school, she fixated on getting as far away from home as possible. The illness her mom faced impacted Angela to develop a thriving state of mind. *"I believed that if I kept myself busy and in a constant state of doing, then I would never be like my mom,"* she recounted.

Angela's thirst for a positive female role model eventually surfaced in her later teens... the mother of her first boy friend. *"She was so different than what I had been exposed to up to this point in my life. She was amazing and full of life so I latched onto her."*

Unfortunately Angela soon uncovered the relationship with her boyfriend wasn't necessarily serving her. *"In retrospect, it was an emotionally unhealthy relationship to be in during that time of my life. I was young and of course I thought I was in love. I lost myself in this rocky and physical relationship. I felt afraid and unable to speak up and honour myself."*

As she fled her home life, she felt she missed out on connecting with her younger sister *Erika*. She expresses feelings of regret from the years of not really getting to know her sister who was nine years younger. *"Like most teenagers my state of consciousness revolved around my own world. Thankfully, my brother Frank was only one year younger, so we spent more time together and even travelled to Europe."*

At a young age, her desire for creating freedom was intense and guided every decision. She had no interest in being *tied down* or playing by someone else's rules. She developed an insatiable appetite for exploring new frontiers and savouring new experiences.

Upon graduating university at the age of twenty-two, she chose to live and work in *Paris* for a year. She even enrolled in linguistic courses at the notorious *Sorbonne* to satisfy her dream of being surrounded in the energy of learning and academia.

At that time, she had little desire to follow her friends who were choosing more traditional and corporate roles. For the first time in her life, Angela gave herself permission to just *be* and savour her one precious life.

"At the time I was fascinated with the world of academia and surrounding myself with growth. I felt like Steve Jobs taking courses that I was passionate about instead of ones that I was made to feel I should take."

"Existing in Paris was playtime for me. I loved spending my days sitting in cafés, visiting museums and soaking in the energy of this majestic part of the world. I felt so alive and free, something that my heart was longing for," she added.

At this point in her life, she had suspended her perpetual state of doing. She was free and discovering new ways to fill up her own cup.

Angela eventually developed a curiosity for *Buddhism*. She was fascinated with growing and expanding her *inner world. "There were a lot of courses I felt I 'should' take in University versus areas*

Women Inspiring Change

of study that fascinated me like Buddhist principles."

She suddenly felt constrained by the energy of what she *should* be doing. She faced emotional struggles like; staying in a relationship that wasn't serving her or undertaking a degree that didn't speak to her soul. She found herself straddling two different worlds. On the one hand, she desired emotional freedom and on the other, a need to conform to societal pressures.

This tug-of-war created an *imbalance* in her mind. She began losing herself from the energy of *pleasing others*. What she longed for was to define herself through a greater sense of freedom and individuality.

~ Inspired Insights ~
INFLUENCERS GO WITHIN

When you find yourself at a crossroads ask yourself:
"Who do I want to be? What actions bring me joy?
What would I regret not experiencing in my life?

As she reflects on her life, she is able to ascertain the deeper learnings from the challenges she experienced with her mom. *"I realize, today, that the journey with my mother is meant to teach me the power of acceptance. For years, I resisted what my mom was going through and how she wasn't emotionally available to me."*

While these challenges influenced Angela to grow into a strong and independent woman, it also came at the expense of a deeper understanding of her inner self. The turbulent relationship with her first boy friend taught her to honour herself.

"All of my relationships including my seventeen year marriage, taught me the importance of honouring my needs and desires instead of just pleasing others."

She learned that by honouring herself she wasn't acting selfishly. Like most people, she was conditioned at an early age to believe that focusing on her own self interests would hurt others.

~ Inspired Insights ~
INFLUENCERS HONOUR THEIR SPIRIT

Focus on honouring your spirit and in that light... you serve your higher self.
When you ignite your inner light you in turn, inspire others to do the same.

Upon returning to *North America* in her 20's, Angela found herself falling back into her perpetual state of doing. Her world now accelerated as a result of managing several jobs. As the world twirled in her mind, her heart savoured a life of freedom like she experienced in *Paris*.

At an ambivalent age of fifty, she finds herself longing to experience that *state of being* she tasted over thirty years ago while existing in the heart of *Paris*. *"Today I have a deep desire to displace this incessant need to be constantly doing. I've been running in that high gear state for most of my life. It's exhausting and it's scary how much of your life you don't even notice when you are in that state."*

With the passing of time, she lives with an intention of slowing

Women Inspiring Change

down to observe her one precious life. She focuses her mental, emotional and physical energy on creating a life of inner peace. As she continues to open her heart to me, I sense a whisper from her younger self craving the same experience.

~ Inspired Insights ~
INFLUENCERS ARE NOT DEFINED BY WHAT THEY DO

Tell yourself that you are enough. You are not defined by what you do. You are a spiritual being experiencing life through a physical body.

You are perfection in all of your imperfection.

Upon returning from *Paris* and after a tumultuous relationship, Angela also felt the need to create a sense of stability in her life. So at the age of twenty-six, she chose to get married, settle herself in a suburban bubble and raise a family.

"At the time I was seeking a complete contrast to my turbulent life. Initially, I found this marriage easy and joyful and the right detour to the life I had driven." Married with children, she found her self being pulled back into a familiar energy of *doing*. Working in a fast-paced world of pharmaceuticals, dropping off and picking up the kids and training early in the mornings, emptied her tank. She found herself exhausted and burnt out.

"It was at this stage in my 30's where I began really noticing how deeply unhappy I was. I noticed the widening disconnection in my marriage and how we both wanted very different things in life. Everyday as I drove into work, I was crying. I no longer recognized

the reflection in the mirror or the life I was living."

~ Inspired Insights ~
INFLUENCERS FAIL FORWARD

Quite often it's the discomfort that becomes the catalyst for explosive growth.

Failing forward creates the space for self-reflection.

Comfort only suppresses our passion for the soul.

This intense discomfort led her to the world of personal development. She always had a keen interest in reading inspirational books so she enrolled in courses and soaked in the energy of personal growth.

"I remember setting a powerful intention after one course. By the time I hit forty, I was going to figure a few things out," she recalled. She was determined to not enter her 40's feeling sad and detached from her inner being that was now busting to emerge.

The more she took 100% responsibility for her life, the deeper her sense of purpose flowed. Her soul was ignited with a new sense of passion. Her thirst in transforming herself from the inside out fuelled her with a new sense of energy.

She rediscovered her passion for fitness and became certified as a personal trainer. Training her body and mind strengthened her resolve to find herself. She loved working with people and helping them create personal goals. While still working as a full time pharmaceutical sales rep, personal training was serving its purpose as a stepping-stone to something more profound.

She was like a treasure hunter on a journey of uncovering a

deeper meaning in her life. She felt the need to excavate new layers of contribution but didn't quite know what the path would be. Her world was opening up and she began attracting an assemblage of personal development coaches.

She was particularly fascinated with one coach, an older gentleman named *John Kanary*. *"He opened my mind to the power of helping others create and experience a better life, the very energy I was seeking."*

~ Inspired Insights ~
INFLUENCERS SEEK FULFILLMENT

The path to greater happiness, fulfillment and purpose is to become the very thing you are seeking. Ask yourself: What do you want others to experience?

At this point, Angela was committed to daily, personal improvement. She was not willing to settle for a mediocre way of existence. She infused personal development into all areas of her personal and professional life. *"I even weaved my newfound awareness into the sales meetings I led and shared the energy with the physicians I called on. I was like a wild animal spewing personal development with anyone that would listen,"* she enthusiastically shared.

This sharing with others ignited the embers of her passion and fuelled her own personal transformation. The sadness that hovered over her like a dark cloud, while driving to visit physicians each day, was replaced with a light of inspiration as she listened to inspiring audio programs. *"I loved filling up my mind with this daily inspiration. I couldn't get enough of these new thoughts."*

Angela was learning to take 100% control of her state by training and conditioning the state of her mind.

She found a way to empower herself and *change her mind.* The more she developed herself the more she recognized not only the mental and emotional disconnect but also the spiritual one that was growing between her and her husband. *"It became clear to me that I had put aside my own deeper needs in order to please and not hurt others in this marriage."*

She intuitively knew that she could not exist in this way of being and within this marriage much longer. It would just be a matter of time that she would find her inner voice and choose to create a new life that filled up her heart, mind and soul.

"When I hit forty, I felt amazing. My transformation was now in full force and I loved reaching this goal that I set a few years ago for myself. My soul-sucking job and my marriage slowly faded into the shadows. My personal training and immersion into personal development became my new light."

It seemed that the more she connected to her *spiritual self* through personal growth the more her marriage unravelled. She continued to enrol into even deeper personal growth courses and found herself answering bigger questions.

"As I began understanding that growth was no longer possible, within the contexts of this relationship, for either one of us, I remember writing down that one day I wanted to experience a new level of physical, emotional, mental and spiritual connection with

Women Inspiring Change

someone. I reflected on this vision often. I fixated on this feeling through my vision boards and in my daily journals."

Angela was ready to welcome the next chapter of her life. It was as if she was feeling her ability to attract what her heart truly desired.

~ Inspired Insights ~
INFLUENCERS MANIFEST WHAT THEY DESIRE

Only you have the power to manifest what you desire most.
By becoming clear on what you desire to experience and fixating on the end result, you attract new energies into your life.

Angela was seeking a deeper connection and believed with every ounce of her being, that the universe would answer her call. She could see clearly now that this longing for a deeper level of *connection* was the key ingredient missing in all of her past relationships.

"I now had a desire to grow with someone in all areas of my life. Visions of reading together in bed, sharing glasses of wine and experiencing growth together, filled my soul. My heart ached for this experience."

Low and behold, the universe answered Angela's call by delivering her the love of her life. A vibrant and explosive being who she sensed, upon their very first encounter, they had danced in the universe together before. *"The synchronicities leading up to this wondrous manifestation were the result of letting go and allowing the universe to deliver,"* she added.

Little did she know that the new love of her life was longing for the exact same experience. *"I love how we came together. We were both coaching at this place called Think Spot, in Burlington. It felt as if this place existed for the singular purpose of bringing us together."*

The more that Angela stepped into embracing this new life, the more challenges she faced. That's the brilliance of the universe. When you focus on change that's when everything changes.

Despite being faced with some of the most difficult challenges in life, she was now ready to run towards her life, to seize it like her life depended on it. Even her husband's unfortunate health diagnosis that posed significant emotional challenges could not keep her, this time, from leaping into her life. *"I felt as if, in that moment, the universe was testing me as to how bad I wanted this new life, I had not been able to leave when it was relatively easy and my husband and I were dividing up the dinner plates together."*

Angela attracted what her heart was longing for. She chose to embrace these new challenges with greater levels of love, empathy and belief. She realized that when life was simple and easy, she wasn't growing. During these arduous times, she courageously found her voice and embraced the love she deserved.

She had spent the past forty years doing and living for others and being what they wanted her to be. She wanted to fall backwards with her arms stretched out wide into the arms of a new life and love. *"Despite the challenges that surrounded me, I wanted to create a life that I could experience...I wanted to reclaim my life,"* she shared.

~ Inspired Insights ~
INFLUENCERS CRAVE CONNECTION

The life that you crave most, requires an unwavering connection to the only thing that matters... listening with the intent to understand the whispers from your heart.

Reflecting on her life journey, Angela was greatly influenced by her father. Despite how hard he worked, he served as a healthy and positive role model in her life. He inspired her to *dream bigger* and create an independent life filled with joy.

"I loved the connection to my dad. He was the dreamer and the entrepreneur that I craved to be. He inspired me to take care of my personal health and what it is to follow your heart in the face of challenge and voices around you telling you to play it safe."

Her Grandfather influenced the magic of seeing the light in someone else and to shine that light brightly even in the face of life's circumstances.

The mother of her first boyfriend, *Mrs. J*, influenced her to be present and find her inner power. *"She was always so positive, present and really listened to me. I loved her fascination and curiosity for all that I was doing and pursuing."*

"In my mid 30's the coaches that I met, like John Kanary, influenced me to follow a similar path. I witnessed that a career in personal development was actually possible. He inspired me to pursue a life of coaching people to create better lives."

The fascination with *Buddhism* influenced Angela's spiritual belief and connection to her role in the universe. She found peace and serenity in visiting a small, local *Buddhist* temple.

"I remember asking the Buddhist monk, Rabgye why I was so drawn to Buddhism. He confidently reassured me that I practiced this art in another life. At once I knew this to be true. I also fondly remember a teaching on death that literally shifted the trajectory of my life. I had been hesitating for years to step into my life when all of a sudden I was hit with a teaching that death is certain and timing is uncertain - so what are we waiting for? This shocked me into life."

This deeper realization of her mortality was rocket fuel for her soul. It influenced where and how she allocated her life energy. *"I began asking myself everyday; 'If I only had one year to live, would I be doing what I am doing now?' I found this to be a very real way to live my life. This new filter for my life helped me tune out the noise and tune in to what really mattered."*

~ Inspired Insights ~
INFLUENCERS EMBRACE THEIR MORTALITY

Becoming awake to the notion of our mortality serves as a tremendous wake up call to step into creating our lives with a greater sense of urgency.

Meditation for Angela has become a powerful way of serving others. For years she was fascinated with helping people elevate themselves in all areas of their life and leadership. *"Today, I choose to focus on this one area; meditation, that positively influences and impacts every aspect of our lives. It does this because it changes the nature of our mind. When you change your mind, you change your life."*

In her previous years of leadership coaching, she always felt as if something was missing in her ability to truly propel people forward in their lives.

"Meditation and mindfulness has become the missing link. I can see clearly now its power to help people calm the state of our brain and mind and connect to their deeper selves. The ability to forge a deeper connection with myself, so that I can really notice and also actively create my one precious life has been what my heart has been longing to experience. I want everyone to experience this power they have within."

As she continues to dive deeper into the *science of meditation*, she finds herself fascinated and influenced by the creative teachings of *Dr. Joe Dispenza, Deepak Chopra* and *David Ji*. *"It's the creative and inspiring way in which they deliver the science that ignites my curiosity and draws me in."*

This energy has ignited her professional practice as a *meditation coach and creator*. She leads with an intention of helping her clients create a new mind to focus on what truly matters and be connected to one's heart in this brief and brilliant lifetime.

During the conception of this book, Angela researched the energy that shapes a person of influence. *"The inspired energy of influence fascinates me. What I've discovered is we tend to view influence as hierarchical thing of position and power as if this energy is reserved for political leaders or people with a certain status. The truest essence of influence is an energy that emanates outward from an inspired state. When one is more deeply connected to the purpose for one's existence, we emit an outflow of energy or influence into the world. I love thinking of influence in this light."*

~ Inspired Insights ~
INFLUENCERS CONNECT WITH THEIR DEEPER WHY

When you experience a deeper connection to yourself and why you exist, you are able to influence others around you just by your very presence.

"I feel as if I'm finally stepping into my inspired influence. When I initially conceived my company 'Focused Energy' years ago, I felt truly 'unfocused'. Today, it feels spectacular to be under the influence of an inspired state and a deeper purpose for why I am really here."

With a shift in her own mindset, she is able to help people create profound change by helping them *really* notice their lives. By changing her mind she was able to change her life.

~ Inspired Insights ~
INFLUENCERS SHAPE THEIR OUTLOOK

The quality of our mind shapes our outlook on the world.
It influences our way of being within it.

Angela has gained clarity for *why she exists*. She is aware of her unique ability to serve others and contribute in meaningful ways to the richness of humanity. She listens and receives feedback from others with an open heart. She knows that her energy, voice and creative approach are helping people connect to what really matters.

Her single-minded intention now flows out effortlessly. She feels that she is improving lives by helping people improve the quality of their minds.

Angela's *top actions* **for stepping into your own influence:**

- Live with a daily intention of growing from everything and everyone that shows up.

- Constantly seek out new ways to improve yourself: physically, emotionally, spiritually and mentally. *"Cultivate daily habits like meditation, body movement, healthy mindful eating habits, listening to inspired audio and reading a piece of inspiration everyday. Turn off the news and surround yourself with positive and inspiring content and practice honouring and protecting yourself from negative energies."*

- Embrace the discomfort that will show up as a result of your willingness to change with intention and action. *"This willingness to grow will ultimately influence the actions."*

- Face all adversities in life with love for yourself and *build the capacity to trust* that the right path and outcomes will unfold.

- Choose to be in a relationship founded on growth. *"I chose to attract and step into a relationship that was more aligned with my values surrounding personal growth and contribution."*

Her influence will be experienced by generations as a woman, mother and life partner who loved experiencing life and inspired others to *step into theirs*. Her children will remember how she celebrated their unique gifts by learning to be fully present in the moments they shared.

Her belief in her *passion* and *purpose* to serve others by improving the quality of their minds, cultivated a deeper connection within a disconnected age. Her intention to help people experience their lives more fully, elevated our world.

Angela has a very strong gift for helping someone embrace their path. *"I know that every footstep has brilliantly unfolded. It brought them to this point and made them who they are. Everything that showed up in one's life is meant to reveal a deeper learning and truth about their path. I try and bring this energy into the personalized meditations that I create for people,"* she enthusiastically adds.

Angela's wish for others is to help them embrace the reality that life *is brilliant and brief. "People tend to fixate on insignificant energy. Our world has forgotten what truly matters. I want to ignite a sense of urgency in people. It is only through this deeper understanding that we will no longer waste a drop of our precious time. If we exist as if we only had one year to live...we would focus only on what brings us joy. This is not reckless living, this is what it means to really live."*

She is filled with epic levels of gratitude for her health and the love in her life and how she gets to spend her days helping others. She serves the world by contributing to a new consciousness. She connects people by shifting their way of thinking about their lives. She creates the way for a new mind that focuses solely on what matters...a world filled with love, meaning and abundance.

Day-by-day, Angela does the work to feel more connected to her *inner self*. She knows that she is surrounded by angels that are helping her uncover the deeper meaning and learnings in her life.

Her life-long journey has inspired her to notice life and experience the presence of all its daily miracles. For the first time in Angela Kontgen's life, she is beginning to feel worthy.

As she pauses to sip her last mouthful of hot tea, I feel her grandfather's energy around her and see him smiling and raising his cup and as he whispered to her, *"You are enough my dearest, you always have been and I love how you are stepping into your light and helping others do the same."*

"DECIDE WHAT YOU WANT MOST, TAKE ACTION AND GO GET IT!"

~ Gerry Visca

Photography by:
Whole Lotta Grace and Nan Deily

5. Jenni Byrd Grier

Live Above Your Current Circumstances

"I exist to help people achieve and grow." ~ *Jenni Byrd Grier*

*L*ike most young girls, Jenni found the years in middle and high school somewhat arduous. She learned early on that she had little desire to follow the crowd. Others criticized and ostracised her desire to create her *own way*. *"I was following what I thought was right... for my heart and I took a lot of hits for that."* She can clearly see now how this way of perceiving the world shaped who she is today.

She isn't someone who beats around the bush. She tends to face most challenges head on...a leadership trait that serves her well. She uncovered her spiritual and steadfast strength through creative avenues like dance and church.

Her training as a dancer elevated her fortitude. Engaging in church youth groups connected with the spirit of her loving and supportive parents. She knew her strength wouldn't materialize from the paltry influence of her high school peers but rather from inspiring outlets.

INFLUENCERS SHAPE THEIR INNER WORLD

Instead of attempting to change others, choose to change the way you look at others.
You only have the power to shape your inner world.

Her mom instilled meaningful lessons of hard work and dedication. At a tender age, Jenni embraced the power of unconditional love to shape her life. *"My mom exemplified unconditional love. Even at her current age of sixty-eight... she can still outwork me. She has more energy and drive than anyone I've ever met,"* she laughingly added. Her mom's nurturing values sculpted Jenni's persona.

Her dad, *David Byrd, is an elite leadership coach* who worked closely with *Paul J. Meyer* as the president of his personal development company. Throughout her life, David served as a source of inspiration and spiritual leadership for their family.

"I love sharing the story of a magazine contest that I won in my sixth grade. Whomever sold the most copies earned a large white fuzzy robot. I wanted this robot really badly and I remember sharing with my dad how I didn't believe I could win."

Her dad in his brilliant wisdom, simply looked at her and said, *"Jenni, if you don't dream big you'll never know what's possible."* Together with her dad, they developed a four week strategic plan for her to sell the most magazines at their office, church and throughout the neighbourhood.

"We started out at his office and to my surprise, I was responsible for approaching every co-worker on my own. Little did I

know my dad influenced me to get out of my comfort zone. For the next three weeks...I followed the plan. I intentionally avoided the distraction from my friends, as I didn't want to know how many copies they sold. At the end of the contest, I won the robot and set the school record for the most magazine sales ever."

Despite winning a pointless robot, this *fuzzy* contest inspired her at an early age that anything is possible when you *dream big*, put a plan in place and take massive action.

~ Inspired Insights ~
INFLUENCERS MARCH TO THE BEAT OF THEIR OWN DRUM

Big Dreamers are not swayed or influenced by the noise of the crowd. They march to the beat of their own drum. They decide what they want most and take powerful action.

Funny enough, her dad didn't even remember this story when she shared it a few years ago on stage. This powerful life lesson at the age of twelve influences her parenting style to this day. *"You never know what memories forged through everyday living, will impact and shape your children's lives,"* she added.

Despite colouring inside the lines, what set her apart from the crowd was her choice to *not* give into peer pressure. Charting her own path helped her stand out, a trait that most people fear to embrace as a result of being ostracised from society.

She intuitively knew that her joy and sense of purpose, materialized through serving others. She tackled several mission trips, including one to Russia even while she was five months

Women Inspiring Change

pregnant. *"My mom thought I was crazy but the Russians took good care of me."*

Being surrounded by her parent's spiritual energy, invoked a deeper calling to serve the world. She cultivated a deeper desire to help others believe in themselves. As a leadership coach, she feels a greater sense of contribution. *"It's as if for the first time in my life, I feel I am doing exactly what I was put on this earth to do."*

~ Inspired Insights ~
INFLUENCERS KNOW THEIR PURPOSE

We are all born with a deeper and more profound purpose.
Life is about uncovering this inner knowing and living your life through it.

Jenni worked in *Corporate America* for eighteen years. Even though she performed admirably and successfully climbed the ladder, she always felt a deeper calling...to serve others. In a sea of unwanted politics she navigated to the activities that filled her with joy like helping her team grow.

Throughout her dubious journey, she found herself questioning the destination. *"I wasn't sure what all the years of hard work was leading me to,"* she recounted. Her uninspiring job responsibilities didn't contribute to the difference she was aching to steer in the world.

"I now recognize the power in that feeling of knowing exactly what you were meant to do in the world. That is why I feel so passionate about helping people reach that same place in their lives."

One of Jenni's favourite quotes by *Author Jerry Sittser; A Grace Disguised* is: *"Faith is believing in advance what only makes sense in reverse."* She believes that most people don't like their challenges. Throughout her journey, Jenni conditioned herself to embrace life's learnings and challenges with ease and grace.

"In the past I often resisted going through my challenges. It's not about liking your challenges in the moment... no one welcomes discomfort. I know that I will learn and grow through an energy of acceptance."

She shared with me the challenge she experienced with her oldest daughter's sensory processing disorder. Jenni's family experienced an unsettling five year journey, battling physicians in an attempt to obtain a correct diagnosis. Essentially, her daughter's nervous system got overloaded resulting in major meltdowns.

Jenni shared how her daughter struggled with any form of change. *"As a parent I often agonized in ascertaining whether this was a discipline problem. The deeper learning in working with an Occupational Therapist (OT), Kristen Oliver, revealed a powerful insight...thoughts have power. Kristen asked me one question that changed my life, "What are you thinking when she has these meltdowns?"*

Their OT, Kristen helped Jenni uncover the thoughts that didn't serve her. *"I realized my daughter could feel the energy of my adverse thoughts. This energy seemed to contribute to the outcomes she was experiencing,"* she adds.

Jenni rose above her current situation. She learned to influence positive outcomes during her daughter's outbursts by channelling new thoughts of positive memories of her as a baby. To her disbelief, the typical sixty minute meltdowns her daughter experienced the past five years, suddenly dissolved after only ten minutes. *"The new outcomes of my daughter embracing me with expressions of love was extraordinary."*

This was a defining moment and transformational experience for her family. She arrived at a profound realization that our thoughts impact the actions of others around us. *"Not so long ago in my unconscious state, my mom recently reminded me of how I didn't handle this challenge with grace and ease. As a stressed out Corporate America executive at the time, I remember thinking...my life sucks,"* she laughingly recounted.

The deeper learnings that she embraced during these challenging times shaped the very way she coaches her leadership clients today.

~ Inspired Insights ~
INFLUENCERS EMBRACE DISCOMFORT

For things to change you need to be the one that embraces discomfort as the ultimate catalyst for growth.

What Jenni now knows for certain is when her energy is in the ideal place; it positively influences her overall home environment. *"I understand and accept the lessons I'm meant to embrace on my journey through life. I know that when I keep my energy in the right place, everything around me changes."*

A full day of coaching and giving to others never prevents her from maintaining a sense of joy and purpose throughout her day. She draws from the inspiration and energy of her clients.

~ Inspired Insights ~
INFLUENCERS DON'T REACT

You relinquish your power the moment you react to someone else's behaviour.
Influencers grow by pausing and reflecting on the teaching in any given moment.

She longed to flourish at any task she was doing. Today, she lives with a stronger desire to connect others, by seeing the potential in one another. *"It is my hope that everyone starts to perceive life as 'incomplete' rather than being wrong! I would love to see people learn to live about their circumstances and not...in them."*

She approaches everyday from a beginner's mind with a thirst for continual growth and learning. *"My dad always says: 'We either grow or decline.' I continue to do what I ask all of my clients...to live above my circumstances and not in them. I know I will face greater challenges in life. It's my goal to handle all of them with grace and ease."*

~ Inspired Insights ~
INFLUENCERS EXPOSE THE PARTS

The good times create an illusion of progress.
It's only through the challenging times that we expose the parts that require our attention.

Jenni existed as an achiever with a *full steam ahead* attitude her whole life. *"I have two gauges, on or off. There is no middle one in there for me."*

Whether she was breaking middle school records or climbing corporate ladders, she mastered the art of doing and achieving. Today, the energy that drives her deeper purpose and curiosity is the collective power of our thoughts and their ability to bind and influence us.

The past two years of her journey, helped crystallize her vision for how she will serve the world. *"It's been a dream of mine my whole life to work with my father in his company David Byrd Consulting. Coming to this greater awareness has just been amazing. This journey has brought me so much more than I could have ever imagined,"* she shared.

She lives a humble life and is often brought to tears when others share testimonials about her. She is filled with gratitude for the life she gets to live. *"Like most of us, I often don't see the gifts in me that others see."*

Recently, I asked Jenni to write a tip on *Leading with Persistence,* for one of my inspiring publications. She laughingly shared how stumped she was and even called her dad for some insight.

He laughed and replied:

"Jenni, you are the most persistent person I know. It comes so naturally that you don't even recognize it."

"It took hearing that to help me realize...it is my gift," she added.

~ Inspired Insights ~
INFLUENCERS UNCOVER THEIR TREASURES

It is often challenging to recognize the unique abilities within ourselves.
We are born with unique talents that others see and experience in us before we do.

Part of the system that *David Byrd* teaches is creating a *five year vision statement.* In 2011, David boldly made the decision to venture out on his own and incorporate his new company, *David Byrd Consulting.*

Witnessing his decision, she knew she was ready for a change. Even though she didn't know when or how it would happen, she had a desire to join him and serve others with her unique gifts.

The stressful demands of her corporate life no longer served her bigger vision. She craved simple pleasures and a life of greater balance. She lavished at the thought of starting each day by taking her kids to school and picking them up from the bus stop.

"Around the same time I wrote out my five year vision statement that I was going to work with David Byrd Consulting, performing coaching calls and helping people reach their next level of success."

To her wonderment, her vision materialized three years later in February 2014. She fixated on her desired vision with powerful intentionality. *"Psychologists revealed that we have a tendency to move in a direction of expectation,"* she added.

Prior to the realization of her vision, she was leading a major team in *Corporate America.* She didn't get hung up on how this new chapter would unfold...she allowed her belief and intention to *write* the way.

Leading up to creating her vision statement, she experienced a dream that revealed she needed to learn her dad's business and teach others his *Next Level Achievement System.* A few months later she revealed her dream of creating a legacy with him. Her dad couldn't believe his ears as he stood there, overcome with great emotion as he lovingly replied, *"Jenni...I prayed for the exact same thing."*

It was as if the energy and love that co-existed between a father and daughter, magnetized their vision. It would take eighteen months to finally implement the plan. It was no longer a matter of when; it was only a matter of time before they joined forces.

From a young age, she experienced life with an inner knowing and a desire to one-day walk hand-in-hand with her dad, serving other people. She was grateful for her previous executive role, yet she never quite felt a sense of peace working in that capacity. *"I wasn't settled in my corporate role and I always knew there had to be more to life. Work-life balance was missing, something that was very important to me."*

She shared a sense of regret in missing out on important things in the first ten years of her eldest daughter's life... while climbing the corporate ladder. *"I was always working and travelling. I never got to take my kids to school or pick them up from the bus stop. I used to get home from my job at 6:00pm,"* she sadly recounted.

Today, she savours the extra two hours from 4:00pm to 6:00pm with her kids. She basks in their energy and the chime that their voices make as they enthusiastically share the events of the day. For Jenni, these magical two hours are like a newfound treasure and a window to her soul.

~ Inspired Insights ~
INFLUENCERS SET POWERFUL INTENTIONS

The universe responds to clarity of thought, expectation and intention. See the very thing you are seeking, believe it's possible, take action and allow it to flow.

Her parents had the greatest impact on her life. They modelled spiritual leadership and unconditional love. She welcomes each day with blessings of gratitude for having them both in her life. *"I've learned so many different things from both of them."*

Her mom's hard work and determination continues to influence her choices in life. *"She's sixty eight and thrives at managing a dental practice. She has more energy than anyone I know. She inspires me to model unconditional love and put family first."*

Her astute dad inspired her as the spiritual leader in the family. He taught her to *dream big* and set herself up to win in life. *"It sounds like such a simple concept but most people condition themselves to lose,"* she revealed. His teachings guided her to live with hope, anticipation and positive expectancy. *"I love the energy of that word 'expectancy' and its power to drive tomorrow forward."*

INFLUENCERS EXPECT GREAT RESULTS

Surround yourself with people who encourage you to dream bigger.
Nurture your relationships and expect greater results in your life.

Everyday people like Jenni, have the potential and the power to become influencers. Some people seize this power while others choose to simply remain in their conditioned comfort zones.

The influencers we admire started out as everyday people who chose to ignite the untapped potential in their hearts. *"They have this heartfelt view that comes from the core of their being and they have to do it. It's this driving vision that allows them to live above their circumstances and not in them. They fixate on what can be instead of what currently is."*

Influencers share three common traits:

1. **Vision** ~ They have a vision for themselves and for the world around them.

2. ***Self Realization*** ~ They know who they are, their purpose and why they are doing it. Influencers are clear on *why* they are here. Their passion and purpose fuels their outcomes.

3. ***They Listen*** ~ Influencers listen to their heart and to their core. They tune out the noise of the crowd.

The following two actions underline Jenni's daily habits:

- She channels the mindful power of her thoughts.
- She implements a practice of daily meditation. *"Thank goodness for my meditation coach, Angela Kontgen,"* she laughingly added.

A powerful leap in her development during these past two years is her driving focus to harness the power of her mind. She is learning to master being mindful of her thoughts. *"Meditation seems to freak a lot of people out. I quiet my mind and become intentional with my thoughts. This helps me draw in what I am focused on creating."* She believes our thoughts create our personal reality so we need to become mindful of what we are thinking. Thousands of thoughts enter our mind on a daily basis. Many of us can't control the influx of these thoughts from our subconscious mind, but we do have the power to choose which thoughts we focus on and our reaction in any given moment.

"Do I believe it or... do I reject it? I have a magnet on my computer that reads: Don't believe everything you think! This has become my new motto," she laughingly shared.

~ Inspired Insights ~
INFLUENCERS THINK ABOUT THEIR LIVES

What you think about all day long is what you bring about in your life.
Your thoughts become things.

Women Inspiring Change

I asked Jenni how her daughters would be impacted by her influence ten years from now. She hopes her daughters will see that her mom lived with intention and an abundance of love. *"I believe that is what life is all about. I recently shared with a client that you need to fall in love with life again. I hope my daughters can use these learnings in her life like I'm starting to use them in mine."*

Jenni has a desire to transcend her understanding of the power of our thoughts to shape our lives. Through her coaching, she is inadvertently impacting her client's children and forging future generations of mindful thought leaders. *"You're right, my clients have shared with me videos of how their kids employ a daily practice of affirmation."*

She shared a story of a recent visualization exercise that she used with her youngest daughter during a soccer tournament. *"Angela Kontgen would be proud,"* she noted.

Her younger daughter was competing earlier that morning and Jenni helped her visualize scoring several goals. *"Driving to the soccer field, I playfully helped my daughter vividly feel the feelings of scoring three goals. Upon arriving, she walked up to her coach and declared with enthusiasm that she was going to score three goals. The first half of the game her team was loosing 3-0 and to the crowds amazement, my daughter scored three consecutive goals in the second half of the game."*

Suddenly, Jenni found herself coaching and training her daughter's friends during the lunch break on the power of visualization. At the end of the game, all three of the young girls had accomplished in the second half of the game what they visualized. *"The coach approached me after the game and jokingly asked if I could help prepare all the kids with a visualization exercise before the start of each game. That's the great thing about kids; they are so open to everything. They don't have all the blocks that adults have."*

~ Inspired Insights ~
CHILDREN ARE OUR GREATEST TEACHERS

They reveal our greatest opportunities for growth.
They know their joy and they live it.

Jenni believes in our collective ability to impact one person at a time. As a trainer and coach, she never became distracted by the amount of people attending one of her events. It makes no difference to her if twenty-five or five hundred people choose to show up at an event. It's not the quantity that accelerates her passion but the quality of the impact she drives into each person.

She practices what she teaches her daughters. Leading up to training, she always meditates and visualizes impacting one person in the audience with her energy. *"It's a daunting task to think about impacting the whole world, so I choose to focus on one person at a time."*

For her, success is about helping one person change their thinking, create a better life and reach new levels. Her goal is to help people become mindful of their lives by thinking proactively instead of reactively. *"Achievement is about getting a little bit better each day."*

Her wish for others is to arrive at a realization of their individual power to change their thoughts. Her purpose is greatly centered on inspiring people to take ownership of their thoughts through mindfulness. *"I've come to appreciate the impact of keeping myself in a good place and the impact my energy has on my immediate family,"* she declared. It's so easy to get thrown off by the energy of events, circumstances and others.

The lessons that she shares in these pages reminds me of the power we have in any given moment. We will never be able to change the way others show up. The power that we do have is how we choose to change the way we look at things. By choosing to live proactively and practice mindfulness, we rise above our current circumstances.

The more she develops her mind the more she is able to appreciate herself from another vantage point.

She shares a powerful story of returning home from a two-day meditation retreat being in a very Zen-like state. Her husband and kids were at a soccer tournament.

She delighted in the quietness of her empty home and chose to sit in peaceful contemplation. As she meditated, she visualized her family embracing her with open arms and snuggling on the couch and reconnecting over a movie. The tranquil and loving vision she was experiencing was suddenly removed when her hungry, irritated and tired family came bursting through the door.

"Let's just say my family was just not in a good place! As a result of meditating all weekend and being in the Zen place of my

mind, I almost had an out-of-body experience, consciously observing myself interacting with my troubled family."

A sense of calm resonated throughout her mind and body. She calmly encouraged her husband to take a nap while she fed the kids. She elevated herself above her current circumstances. By preparing her mind in advance she was able to circumvent the frenetic energy she encountered. *"I got to witness how my energy influenced three individuals. Within thirty minutes, everyone around me was suddenly happy and in a good place."* She laughingly shared how that mystical power doesn't happen on a day-to-day basis. That unforeseen event, revealed her power to control her thoughts. It reaffirmed her resolve to help others rise above their current circumstances.

She believes the energy of *influence* is a two-way street driven through a belief in others and listening with the intent to understand. *"You have to meet people where they are at. I never lead with any agendas during my coaching calls."* By leading with an open heart and a mind of acceptance, she helps people grow from where they are.

Similar to *football* players, she revealed how we all need a *helmet in life.* She believes that human beings are not instinctively encouraged to grow. *"Our natural human instincts fight to keep us exactly where we are...in our comfort zones."*

Her training and coaching stems from the premise that achievement and success do not reside within these erroneous zones.

"We have to get uncomfortable to reach that next level. That is where I believe a system of personal management is so vital," she added.

Together with her dad, they teach others to create a proactive mindset through his *Next Level Achievement System.* They encourage others to adopt simple yet highly effective strategies like:

- Create a five-year vision statement.
- Plan out tomorrow before tomorrow begins.
- Plan out next month before next month begins.

"It's this commitment to living with a proactive system that becomes your helmet in life and helps you stay in your right brain." Upon ushering her clients into a proactive mindset, she then helps them understand how their thoughts have power. *"You cannot be in your feelings and proactive state simultaneously,"* she added.

~ Inspired Insights ~
INFLUENCERS ARE PROACTIVE

Belief combined with consistent and proactive action will help you create your desired life.

Jenni Byrd-Grier's legacy of influence will rise above the noise of the crowd. She will continue inspiring everyday people to do what they love by following their heart. Together with her father, they will influence generations of people to be mindful of their choices, moment-by-moment so they can live above their circumstances. She nurtures herself, her mind and all those closest to her with a sense of ease and grace.

As we near the end of our time together, a vision of love and light dances through my mind as I visualize Jenni dashing to the bus stop and embracing her children with loving arms and an open mind.

"**YOU ARE NOT YOUR PAST. YOU ARE WHO YOU CHOOSE TO BE NOW...**

...PUSH BEYOND THE PAIN AND DO WHATEVER IT TAKES TO LIVE YOUR INFLUENCE."

~ Gerry Visca

6. Nathalie Plamondon-Thomas

Think Yourself™ Over It!

"I exist to help people discover themselves."
~ Nathalie Plamondon-Thomas

*W*here most people would see challenges Nathalie Plamondon-Thomas chooses to see opportunities. She lives life with epic doses of positivity. She grew up as a small town girl in *Quebec*.

Looking back on her life, she can quickly ascertain the teachings from any event or circumstance that entered her path. Even throughout her middle school years, she managed to transform the energy of being bullied into a positive learning that has shaped her powerful mind.

She shared with me the intensity of thriving as a leader in the fitness industry for more than three decades. Over ten years ago she captured countless awards such as instructor of the year in Canada. Despite these glowing accolades there was something profoundly missing in her life. *"I thought to myself; now what do I do?"*

At the time of this interview, Nathalie had been asked to write a chapter on *'overcoming adversity'* for another book. *"I proceeded to ask my husband what should I write about considering I lacked challenges my whole life. He laughingly responded: 'My dear, should*

I remind you that you have a brain tumour?' Oh yes, that's right. I completely forgot."

She continues to receive treatment for a brain tumour she was diagnosed with over four years ago. Nathalie is very conscious of the thoughts that she focuses on. She intentionally blocks out any negative energy that could potentially hold her back from thriving in her life.

She was raised in a very positive and loving environment. Her decisive upbringing continues to influence the way she approaches any life adversity. *"Instead of attending church on Sundays, my parents made me sit through hours of motivational tapes like: Zig Ziglar and Og Mandino. They inspired me to view challenges as an opportunity to grow stronger."*

When challenges surface in Nathalie's world she perceives the experience through a different lens. She regards everything as an incredible opportunity for growth. This energy of adversity that seems to shackle most people is an elusive concept to her. *"When I'm speaking to an audience and I observe someone crossing their arms, I just assume they are cold. I don't see challenge and adversity in others. We are constantly making up stories anyways, might as well make up something that serves us, right?"*

As a young girl she chose to experience life's peaks and valleys from a different vantage point. This way of viewing the world often isolated her from friends. Instead of allowing herself to feel ostracised by the energy of others, she found comfort by being with herself. She discerned her conscious isolation as an opportunity to work harder and even advanced a full year as a result.

"I never looked at my early years in the school playgrounds as 'being bullied'. I loved feeling less distracted by the energy of my friends. It allowed me to spend more time during recess and lunch hours excelling at my homework."

This profound shift in mindset helped her leap forward in school and forged new levels of free time to master the art of developing herself. She advanced quickly in high school and earned straight A's in all of her subjects. In university she simultaneously completed two bachelor degrees.

~ Inspired Insights ~
INFLUENCERS FAIL BETTER

The greatest opportunity for personal growth stems from our willingness to embrace the deeper learning inherent within the challenges we face.

Nothing seems to hold this No.1 best-selling author back. Not even a brain tumour! *"It's not that I don't feel challenges. I just choose not to remain stuck there."* Most people spend a majority of their time needlessly worrying about things that will never come to fruition. Nathalie chooses to channel her precious energy in the most productive way that yields exceptional results.

"It's about allocating your time to what truly matters instead of wasting it on inconsequential things. Over 30% of the stuff that most people worry about already happened in the past so no amount of thinking will change that," she added.

She practices what she preaches to her clients. Nathalie has conditioned herself to focus her powerful mind on the things that truly matter. *"Our minds and bodies are constantly aiming at creating a blueprint for our ideal health. The key is to listen to the messages and signals that our brain sends us like: slowing down or focusing more. When we ignore these internal insights that's when ailments show up in our lives."*

She is fascinated with how our bodies and brains are wired to heal us daily. *"We don't have to remind ourselves to heal. Our bodies marvellously do that for us."*

~ Inspired Insights ~
INFLUENCERS FOCUS ON WHAT THEY WANT TO EXPERIENCE

Influencers decide what they want to experience most so they can make time for what truly matters. They are not easily distracted or taken off track as a result of their laser focus. What you choose to focus on expands. Energy flows where your attention goes.

Upon being diagnosed with a brain tumour she listened to the whispers from her body and made significant changes to her lifestyle. In the past, she found herself saying yes to everything as a result of her energy and inspired enthusiasm. Today, her new filter helps her be more selective as to where she channels her precious energy. *"The diagnosis four years ago has helped me funnel my energy to what makes sense and matters most to me."*

She contemplated the bigger questions like:

- What are my values?
- What is non-negotiable?
- What is my purpose?

"Contemplating these big questions really helps me determine where my energy needs to flow."

She uses this simple filtering system to focus on what brings her bliss and the people she serves with her deeper purpose. Nathalie is driven by contributing the most impactful influence she can have on others. This way of being has ignited her life purpose to help others 'think' differently'. *"I love using this filtering system every time someone approaches me with a request. It makes my decision making so much easier. I don't need to say yes to everyone or be involved with everything to experience joy."*

~ Inspired Insights ~
INFLUENCERS LIVE THROUGH THEIR BLISS

Influencers allocate energy only to the actions that bring them tremendous joy and that are aligned with their intention to serve others.

She lives with a *certainty* that she could become whatever she conceives. She never allowed her current circumstances or 'perceived reality' to restrict her unbridled potential of impacting lives. She exists with absolute clarity and belief that human beings can achieve anything they set their minds to.

Women Inspiring Change

"It's easy to become discouraged and hold yourself back by comparing yourself to others. Too many people think about the qualities that they lack. The key is to focus on uncovering the unique characteristics that you admire in others then model their approach."

It's living with an open-ended level of wonderment that continually allows Nathalie to challenge her potential. *"I look at the qualities that I admire in others with curiosity. As long as it's serving my higher purpose, then I uncover the way to make it happen."*

~ Inspired Insights ~
INFLUENCERS ARE DRIVEN BY THEIR PURPOSE

The actions and choices that influencers make in life are discerned by their level of contribution. They are driven by their deeper purpose to serve others through their bliss.

Throughout her teens she continued living the successful habit of listening to motivational programs and modeling successful people. *"Growing up in Quebec City my mom often shared with me valuable insights like: You can't put your hand in a bucket of glue without some of that glue sticking so be careful which bucket you put your hand in."*

Her mothers' influence certainly *stuck* with her. As a young business owner, Nathalie strengthened her mind by reading autobiographies of successful and famous people.

Her mother owned and operated two printing manufacturing plants so Nathalie continually sought out new ways to improve their business. She researched and read about successful *young* entrepreneurs. When she was only twenty years old she was responsible for managing a staff of twenty-five employees in a small town of ten thousand people. She expanded her keen interest in modelling the actions and thinking that young successful entrepreneurs embraced.

"Despite the extraordinary experience with managing a successful facility with twenty-five staff, I remember thinking to myself; I'm not where I should be." She desired to make a greater impact and chose to relocate to the larger plant in *Quebec City* gaining a fresher experience in marketing and sales, impacting over seventy-five employees.

No matter how much knowledge she acquired through her increased responsibilities, she craved larger and more fulfilling platforms to apply her unique gifts. In the evenings she continued teaching fitness classes as a powerful way to augment her day-to-day managerial tasks. As she now approaches her 30th year teaching fitness she joyfully reflects on how she continually sought out new ways to influence people. It was this burning curiosity to help people improve their *thinking* that *stuck* to her like glue.

"Managing staff is one thing but teaching others through fitness and nutrition really helped shape my approach towards inspiring others to be their best. I was even able to transfer this knowledge of personal development into my mother's business."

She knew that her sales and marketing team would eventually plateau if they weren't progressing their mind and body. She learned from her mother how to develop a keen sense of improving the quality of her staff's approach towards happiness.

Eventually all of her families' hard work paid off. The purchase arrangement required herself, her mother and brother to work with the new owners for two years helping transition the innovative systems, strategies and mindset that Nathalie helped cultivate, following her mother's path.

She had a taste of being an entrepreneur so following the two years transition she was focused on creating the next explosive chapter of her life. She expanded her passion for fitness and nutrition by adding: coaching, speaking and authoring books to her personal development repertoire.

Throughout our time together I asked Nathalie what she longed to be in the world during those earlier transformative years of her life. She shared that she was seeking a *deeper awareness* of her life purpose which she defined as 'helping others.' She shared with me a series of profound insights that she learned to master while attempting to unwrap this deeper level of awareness.

"There are many levels and layers within in our brain that we need to navigate. We need to understand how the following layers influence and shape our identity:

- *Your physical environment*
- *Your behaviours*
- *Your skills*
- *Your beliefs and values*

All these layers influence our personality. Beyond this level lies our life purpose. Before you can reach this level you need to address this identity. This happens by being your best and loving yourself."

"In order to make a greater impact on people I didn't believe at the time that I was functioning at my best self. This deeper awareness influenced me to work on my inner self," she recounted.

This epiphany occurred in her twenty-eighth year upon relocating to *Toronto* where she eventually met *Maureen (Mo) Hagan* and the vast world of *Goodlife Fitness*.

"Meeting Mo had an epic impact on my life and ignited a desire to improve myself by navigating these layers and going beyond my identity."

The expanding fitness industry would serve as her global platform. Nathalie became a team leader. She mentored over twenty fitness instructors and was quickly recognized as the top fitness instructor in Canada by *GoodLife Fitness*.

"It was at that point when I decided to focus on making others better. It was no longer about me being my best. I chose to refocus and channel the amount of hours I spent training myself towards helping others."

~ Inspired Insights ~
INFLUENCERS FOCUS ON OTHERS

Your life takes on greater meaning when you flow your energy on improving other people's lives. Influencers focus on creating the 'outcomes' they wish others to experience.

This new mindset of 'serving others' was a major catalyst in Nathalie's expanding world. What I've come to appreciate is when you focus your desire on what you want to create most in life then the universe responds in miraculous ways.

While vacationing in the *Barbados* for three weeks, Nathalie tore her hamstring on the first day running on the beach. She was unable to walk for the remainder of her holiday. She shared how being confined to a wheelchair was the best thing that happened to her. *"It gave me the opportunity to read the book: 'A New Earth' by German-born author Eckhart Tolle about freeing yourself from your 'ego'."*

She experienced a profound and transformational shift during those three weeks. *"It occurred to me that I was way too competitive. I now understood that to make a greater impact on others then my ego had too subside,"* she laughingly shared.

Her inability to walk somehow humbled and healed her. She developed a greater sense of awareness as to how her highly competitive spirit created adversity in her friendships. She recognized that competition drove her to new levels, however her ego wasn't serving her new world. She was determined to balance the qualities of her 'winning' sprit by serving others with a more open heart. *"I recognized that I no longer needed the light to shine on me. I had a new desire to illuminate others."*

This 'new way of being' reduced the stress in her life and helped her feel more at ease with herself. Interestingly, two years later she was nominated for Canada's Instructor of the year again without even pursuing it. She made it to the top five and arrived with a far more humbling spirit as a result of Nathalie just being her natural self.

~ Inspired Insights ~
INFLUENCERS SURRENDER THEIR EGO

"Because of its phantom nature, and despite elaborate defense mechanisms, the ego is very vulnerable and insecure, and it sees itself as constantly under threat. This, by the way, is the case even if the ego is outwardly very confident."

~ Eckhart Tolle

Nathalie had many influencers throughout her life but her mother is clearly cemented in her mind. *"She has this incredible way of always being there and a powerful way of listening to me with the desire to understand. Even though she worked hard she was always present for my brother and I."*

Her mom taught her that she could be a strong and disciplined businesswoman and yet still exude a tender and loving energy towards others. *"I often share that my mom had an iron hand in a velvet glove. She leads her life with an authoritative finesse. She is the most amazing woman I know."*

Mo Hagan continues to serve as a great influence in Nathalie's life. That sense of *certainty* came to the light the moment she met the *Global Fitness Ambassador*. She recalls that 'light of knowing' exploding to life at *canfitpro* in *Toronto*; one the largest fitness expo's in *North America*. She witnessed Mo's desire to break the *Guinness World Record* for the largest 'spin class' ever held.

"I love Mo's determination. She had the room filled with enough spin bikes to beat the world record. Yet with only thirty minutes to go she needed way more people. Everyone around Mo congratulated her for at least trying yet Mo wasn't prepared to fail. With a sense of sheer determination she encouraged everyone in the room to go forth and pull people from off the street in order to fill the room."

Mo's sense of certainty that she would not fail influenced Nathalie at whole new levels. *"Despite the challenge I witnessed how she pulled everyone together. She filled up the spin class in less than thirty minutes and broke the world record! Mo is that woman who makes things happen and doesn't take no for an answer,"* she enthusiastically shared!

~ Inspired Insights ~
INFLUENCERS LIVE WITH CERTAINTY

Influencers live with a sense of certainty for what is truly possible.
They create their own sense of reality and persevere in the face of obstacles.

Influencers help people find their own way. They don't preach from a mountain top but rather inspire others to look up a bit higher and make the climb when they are ready. They have a unique and 'non-invasive' way of wetting people's appetites with their ideas and beliefs.

Nathalie believes the true magic of influencers extends far beyond raising awareness. *"It's their ability to seed new ideas and drive action through powerful thinking,"* she added.

The dream that lives and breathes in Nathalie's heart stems from a world that realizes their full potential. She imagines people waking up to the magic of life and discovering their own special gifts. She has a desire to help people change the way they think in order to transform their outer world.

"We all have a different way of seeing things through our logical and unconscious minds." She recognizes that the true power of transformation does not come from *negative stories* that live in our logical mind but rather through the untapped power of our unconscious mind.

She lives her dream by helping others tap into the power of the most powerful structure of the universe: our brain. *"When people learn to tap into the power of their minds, they can succeed."*

Her transformative work is intended to help people dig into the complex layers of their mind by changing the way they think. *"There is a personal assistant in our mind taking notes and delivering our orders everyday. The key to shifting our minds is to be more aware of the way we think and feel about ourselves. Eventually this inherent programming flows naturally and allows us to succeed,"* she shared.

~ Inspired Insights ~
INFLUENCERS THINK DIFFERENTLY

The thoughts you choose has everything to do with how creative and successful you will become. Change your focus in order to change your attitude towards life.

Through the teachings of her *DNA System* as a Speaker, Life Coach and the wide array of *'THINK Yourself*™' publications including: *THINK Yourself*™ *THIN and THINK Yourself*™ *SUCCESSFUL,* she is focused on helping people transition their lives by programming their own brain.

The following summarizes Nathalie's *top tips* for becoming someone of influence:

- *Develop* a sense of *certainty* and *self-confidence* that you can be your best regardless of external circumstances. Your power lies within you.

- *Seek out* the *learnings* from your past outcomes in order to improve your future actions. Grow from these lessons.

- *Choose* to be *significant* by living a life of contribution and service to others. Reach out and help others feel that they are not alone. This act strengthens your self-confidence.

- *Love* everyone and everything around you in order to receive the love you deserve.

Not everything and everyone that enters our lives are meant to last. As we continue pushing the human race forward by growing our higher selves we can recognize that people and circumstances are often placed in our path for a brief moment in time. The key is to recognize the synchronicity of these events and bless them all with love and light as you continue on your path in becoming your best self.

Nathalie hopes her influence will live on and impact many generations through her *Think Yourself* movement. She has a powerful desire to help people understand that their life is a series of incremental steps moving them along their journey. *"When people detach from the outcomes of these incremental stepping stones they unfold a much bigger part of their lives. Many people think their current way of being is cast in stone but it's not."*

Nathalie is a light and a gift in this world encouraging people to think about their higher selves and their deeper role in the multiverse. This is certainly an influencer who has had a sticky impact on my life.

7. Christy Press

Breaking the Mold

"I exist to inspire human kindness." ~ Christy Press

*C*hristy Press grew up on a farm in *Oregon*. She was a diamond in the ruff. Her dad was her hero and worked hard as a police officer to provide for the family. As the oldest daughter of three, she matured quickly and took responsibility for all household and cooking duties when her mother was ill, which was often.

Like most kids, she wanted to fit in and hang out with the popular girls. Despite her efforts she never quite felt that she was enough. The pressure of 'fitting in' followed her throughout her younger years and into high school.

"I was different than the other girls. I didn't get to have many sleep over's. I loved riding horses and never wore makeup or designer clothes. Unlike the other kids, I didn't get picked up and dropped off by my parents. I was forced to take the bus to school."

Christy struggled to uncover her own identity. She grudgingly fit in with others by existing as a chameleon. *"I thought that's what others wanted from me. I focused on pleasing everyone else. I learned how to be like others but never truly uncovering the real me."*

Unable to control the rage that intensified during her freshman year, her parents were forced to relocate Christy to three different schools. Despite being expelled for fighting, a strong foundation still existed at home.

She was regarded by her mother as; 'her million dollar girl'. Christy lived with a long-held desire to be perceived as a good person. She obsessed in pleasing others in order to attract friends.

With a growing rebellious spirit she was determined to carve out her own independence. She fell in love at a young age and was eventually kicked out of her home at seventeen. A year later she abandoned her long-held desire to study fashion design at the *Art Institute of Seattle,* to marry her boyfriend and become a young mom.

Despite putting her dreams on hold, she was optimistic about raising a family. *"At the time, the traditional mindset was to get married, have kids and raise a family. That's the lifestyle I knew."*

Although Christy followed a traditional path as a result of her conditioning, she envisioned a different future for herself. She visualized working in the high rise towers of *New York* as a successful CEO for a global company. *"I knew at the time that none of my actions were going to get me there. I knew that I needed to make a change."*

At the age of eighteen she intuitively knew she was going to make an impact on people's lives. *"I didn't know how but I believed someday I would make a significant difference in others."*

~ Inspired Insights ~

INFLUENCERS CAST THEIR DREAMS INTO THE WORLD

We are all born as Big Dreamers. This desire burns within each one of us.
Our dreams take flight when we cast it out of the shadows and into the light.

Despite following in her families' footsteps she rides with a sense of pride having been the first female of five generations to graduate from high school. With every stride forward, Christy believed there was a brighter future waiting for her on the horizon. She was determined to break the mold and carve out a new reality for herself.

"I kept telling myself I was going to be bigger than just existing as a mom. I knew I had a ticket to being someone amazing."

At the age of nineteen she faced growing challenges and abusive relationships head on. She found herself hopelessly falling into an adult world without a net. Without a clearly defined way, she found herself making bad decisions. Even though it didn't feel right she worked diligently to maintain a failing marriage.

"I found myself being influenced by his perception of me. The more I heard that I wasn't good enough the more I tried to become what my husband wanted."

Like dirty dishes in the sink, her challenges kept piling up. Whatever self-esteem existed quickly drained away.

Looking back as a proud mother of five, she recounts not being able to stand up to her abusive husband as a result of not knowing who she was. After witnessing him abuse their child she finally summoned the courage to leave her marriage.

Little did she know that listening to the external noise silenced the inner freedom she was seeking. *"When you don't know who you are it's easy to be influenced by others."*

Christy found herself falling into her pre-conditioned pattern and quickly attracted a second blended marriage. *"Instead of searching for inner love I found myself wanting a dad for my kids and someone else I could please. This relationship eventually became the catalyst for the person I am today,"* she recalled.

~ Inspired Insights ~
INFLUENCERS DEFINE THEIR INNER BEING

Influencers go within to define themselves. When you are crystal clear on who you are then you become who you were born to be.

For the next eight years she lost herself even more deeply by becoming what her second husband wanted her to be. This abusive and controlling marriage eventually took its toll on Christy both mentally and emotionally. *"I learned how to hide my voice in order to keep the peace. The only existence I knew was survival mode."*

As she approached the age of thirty she experienced a sudden shift. She came to a profound realization that she was meant for more and ready to cash in her ticket for success. *"It hit me like a ton of bricks. I can't be with this man for the next fifty years of my life! I knew I was not meant to live with this kind of abuse. I was fed up with exposing my kids to this beastly lifestyle,"* she recounted.

Facing the embarrassment of a second failed marriage she found herself torn as a result of loyalty. The relationships she attracted didn't honour the courageous and thriving spirit that existed within her.

Looking back on her life she is able to ascertain the greater learnings. *"I learned that the power of self-worth silences the external noise. Showing up to please others didn't serve my higher self. It only brought me sadness and misery. I learned how to be my own advocate and crush my fears."*

By summoning her inner strength she broke the abusive chains that pinned her down. The fear of surviving gave her the will to fight for her life. With the support of her mother and father she scrambled to find a new home for her and the kids. *"I believe everything happens for a reason. I learned how to claim my life, love myself and become a better mom."*

She longed to find herself and ignite the things that fired her up. *"I felt like the actress Julia Roberts in the movie Run Away Bride. The ending scene where Julia finally discovers the type of eggs she likes. For so many years I didn't even know what kind of music I liked. I was too busy listening to everyone else's noise."*

She finally uncovered her desires and delighted in the melody of making her own decisions. She listened to the whispers of her heart and discovered her purpose in a sea of emotional and abusive chaos.

She chose to look upon herself as being worthy of love and deserving of a better lifestyle. She made the conscious decision to receive love. *"I never heard the words that I was 'beautiful and loving' so I chose to love myself and listen to my inner voice. I decided this was how I was going to be."*

She fixated on the horizon and refused to let her past hold her back from moving forward. She reconnected with the dreams and aspirations of her younger self. Her past journey served as a contrast to the wider path she desired to run.

~ Inspired Insights ~
INFLUENCERS LISTEN TO THEIR INSIDE VOICE

When you dance to the tune of your inside voice you experience the sweet melody of truly living your one precious life.

Today, she longs to define a new level of success in all areas of her life. She desires to inspire her five children ranging from ages two to twenty-two, to believe in themselves. *"I want others to define their own level of success, whatever that looks and feels like,"* she added. She has an intention of influencing women that have lost themselves along their journey as caregiver to their kids and husbands.

Christy's transformation didn't happen over night. She surrounded herself with the wisdom and support of others. She underwent counselling for battered women. *"At the time it was raw and embarrassing. I felt vulnerable sharing my story. I felt powerless and a deep sense of empathy for the other helpless women in the room,"* she openly shared. She shifted from being a victim to an empowered *Goddess*. She held on to the thought of her legacy and the strength and determination she wished to be remembered for.

~ Inspired Insights ~
INFLUENCERS LIVE FOR TODAY

Knowing that you will die is the best way to live your life NOW with no regrets.

Listening to her remarkable story, I sensed Christy's delight in the gift of waking up and seeing the potential of her one precious life. She severed the habitual pattern of losing herself in a string of unhealthy relationships.

Her parents influenced the early part of her life that she could rise above her circumstances. They demonstrated positive values and the fundamentals of a hard work ethic. Their caring nature inspired her to demonstrate empathy for others. *"My parents motivated me that through belief I could be anything I chose to be. Witnessing the 'silent' pain my mother experienced, inspired me to find my voice and not live with regret."*

Musicians like *Madonna* and *Cher* rocked her with their provocative nature and authentic confident persona. This energy influences the way Christy lives out her 'real' life. She knows who she is and doesn't sugar-coat it for anyone. *"When Madonna and Cher hit the stage they owned it! They had no shame or body image issues. They didn't care what other people thought."*

Christy has a long-held desire to inspire women with her voice and her story as a tool to help them carve out their own courage. *"I thought to myself; if Madonna and Cher can do this then I can do it!"*

She perceives and values authenticity, humility and service to others as the primary characteristics of influencers. *"It's the 'realness' in people that inspires me. They don't want anything from you. They see you for you. This is the kind of influence that lives within me. Be whatever you desire to be without the permission from others."*

Christy embraced the following *actions* that sparked her reinvention:

- Her three kids served as a lens for her decision making. *"I thought about the way my kids would see themselves. How would they think and act in a similar situation? How would my boys treat women in the future?*

- She enrolled her kids and herself in counselling.

- She surrounded herself with a myriad of self-help books and created a positive, peaceful and nurturing home environment. *"We didn't watch any violent TV shows. Instead, we filled our minds with happy and fun-loving stories."*

- She focused on being 'the best mom' by demonstrating a positive mindset to her children. She walked the talk and instilled new levels of belief in them and in herself. *"I flooded my mind with positive self-talk. These seemingly simple actions were monumental shifts in my life. I focused on creating a peaceful, connected and healing environment."*

- She learned to put up boundaries and not allow others to dictate her life. *"As I stepped into living these daily actions, my thoughts changed."*

Life still hits her and there are times when she loses her sense of self. However, no matter what changes Christy faces in her personal and professional life, she is able to rise above her current circumstances. *"I'm human like everyone else but with new wisdom, I've learned to embrace and accept the changes. Things happen for a reason and I ask myself; what am I grateful for in this moment?"*

~ Inspired Insights ~
INFLUENCERS WELCOME DISCOMFORT INTO THEIR LIVES

Influencers accept discomfort as a precursor to growth. They see change as stepping stones along the path of their miraculous journey.

She desires to see her influence 'rock on' to the next generation. She wants to be perceived as the new *'Cher and Madonna'* of the business world who lived life on her terms without the need for permission or external validation. *"I want others to see I had a great time in owning my own decisions,"* she laughingly added.

She desires to influence the next generation to *break the mold* and be who they are instead of following what others want for them. *"I love how my seventeen year-old son sees himself owning his own business and becoming a millionaire. My actions inspire him to live on the edge, go after his dreams instead of following a safer and traditional 9-5 path."*

Christy didn't just change her life; she owns it! She had a belief that she was put on this earth for a bigger reason. A small town girl who lived on a farm and experienced a journey through hell was able to consciously change herself towards a life of heavenly fulfillment.

"There is a misconception in others that success happens over night. It's about getting real with the world and revealing the hardship behind the curtain. When we witness the 'real' struggle like I had to face we inspire others that change is universally possible. We don't need to shy away from things like failure when we know it's a precursor to success."

Christy's wish for others is to find joy in being themselves. Believing in human kindness feeds her soul. *"It's about being ok with who you are. We've all suffered. When everyone steps back and extends empathy towards one another then we will inspire new levels of human kindness."*

The following summarizes Christy's *top tips* for becoming a person of influence:

- Accept yourself for who you are.
- Do a self-check by asking yourself: *Who am I? Am I being the person I want to be or am I trying to be someone else?*
- Decide to take 100% responsibility for creating the life you dream about.
- Stop wishing for *someday* and take daily incremental action *today* towards creating your dream life.

- Inspire others with your belief.
- Live with a sense of understanding and compassion for others and strive to raise the level of human kindness in the world.

~ Inspired Insights ~
INFLUENCERS CARVE OUT THE TIME

Influencers carve out the time everyday towards creating their desired life.
Inch-by-inch move yourself towards the direction of your dreams.

"Why can't I? That's the question that I ask myself! I see so many people live with a limiting belief in their ability to invoke change. Instead why not choose to believe that you are good enough and meant for more. Choose to inspire one person with your belief," she shared.

As we near the end of our interview I asked her to envision her influence rippling out into the world and what her kids would say one hundred years from now? An emotional Christy shared with me how important this book is to her. Since the age of fifteen she dreamed of someone publishing her story.

She hopes her courage in climbing out of the depths of hell inspires her kids to climb their own mountains with greater belief and character. She can rest peacefully knowing she paved the way for them to define their own level of success.

She visualizes her daughter existing as a successful heart doctor, her son to be an entrepreneur and making his millions as he speaks about it now, all at the young age of seventeen years old.

Women Inspiring Change

Her oldest son pursuing his dreams as a successful *US Marine*. Her two youngest boys will grow up in love and know success can be self-made, just like mom. She delights at the thought of generations carrying the torch of influence and inspiring their grandchildren with the love she breathed into their hearts.

"It's my greatest wish for others to believe that through every challenge you can choose to rise above it. With belief, hard work and kindness you can inspire change throughout humanity."

She lived with an inner knowing that she was meant for more. She believed in reclaiming a life of independence. She chose to take 100% responsibility for her actions. Her courage and search for self-love became the catalyst for her personal reinvention. Through a relentless belief in her own purpose to inspire change, Christy Press is influencing an energy of 'real belief' in others.

147

"LOOK FOR THE LOVE INSIDE AND YOU'LL ATTRACT WHAT YOU LOVE."

~ Gerry Visca

Photography by: Jon Abeyta

8. Jane Freres

Find Your Voice of Love

"I live to inspire others to love themselves." ~ Jane Freres

*J*ane was a painfully shy girl growing up in a professional home in her small rural town of *Oregon*. Despite being surrounded by an outgoing family and a brother who became a doctor, she struggled in engaging and speaking with adults.

"Although my shyness brought a lot of challenges it also became the catalyst for my reinvention around the age of forty-five." This shyness followed her throughout high school.

Between the ages of twelve and fourteen, she summoned the courage to work in her father's optometry clinic. Still, striking up conversations with adults outside of work, proved to be an arduous task. She was paralyzed at the thought of having to interact with other adults.

She recalls a memory of being in a small store in her hometown and hiding in the aisle of a local store after seeing an adult friend of her parents. *"At that time I would do anything to avoid having to converse with adults other than my immediate family,"* she recalled.

Since the age of ten, Jane had a long-held desire of becoming a mother. The lessons she learned on her journey of discovering herself, taught her to have greater compassion for others.

She has proudly raised her children to harness their voice and believe in who they are. *"This journey has taught me that being shy is more painful than the process of overcoming it."*

Jane experienced a stressful childhood as a result of feeling alone. She witnessed the long tireless hours her mother spent working. *"My mother wasn't as available to me as I would have liked. She was too busy and overworked to spend time and have a deep conversation with me. I longed to have someone that would really listen to me."*

Her mom often said no to things, rather than taking time to know the details. From the age of eight to sixteen, she even contemplated running away. She found herself doing things behind her mother's back like hiding food in the basement as a child in preparation to running away. She believes these are things she normally wouldn't have done had her mom taken time to really listen to her.

"I remember the feeling of being in high school and wanting to live with my friend's family. I wanted to fill up the 'big hole' of loneliness that existed inside of me." She eventually got her wish of being on her own after graduating high school at seventeen and attending college.

Speaking up in her home was never an issue, however through her journey she continued to struggle in finding her voice as she graduated from college and got married. Her desire to run away from home followed her into her college years.

She found herself engaged in her freshman year, married by the time she was eighteen and divorced just three years later. She attracted an older man who had a job and a steady income. *"At the time I longed to be cared for. This yearning resulted in making poor choices in my life. Despite my mother's strong recommendation, I didn't have the voice to unwind this relationship I had started."*

~ Inspired Insights ~
INFLUENCERS SHARE AND TELL

When we don't share our voice then the world is unaware of our special gifts.
Living in silence so others won't feel inadequate, will not connect the world.

Looking back, she embraces the gift of strength and the work ethic her mother gave her throughout her challenging younger years. Jane admires her personal transformation and the strength that now resonates inside of her as a loving parent.

She learned to flow her confident energy into her children. *"I was focused on channelling the adversity I experienced growing up into a new positive way as a parent. Growing up with my mother, made me increasingly aware that children need to be heard and loved in every situation."*

Despite the presence of any bad behaviour, she never let her kids go to sleep without knowing how unequivocally loved they were. *"It's such a simple yet highly impactful habit to create. I feel people miss this essential piece."*

Women Inspiring Change

INFLUENCERS INSPIRE CHANGE

Inspire the change you wish to see in others by becoming the very thing you are seeking to experience.

In her second marriage, her husband was an executive who was invited to many social events. *"I remember saying to him in the car prior to walking into any social event; Please do not leave me alone."*

Jane couldn't imagine walking into a room of strangers and striking up conversations of anything other than her children. This increased level of shyness created higher levels of stress in her life. She found her husband taking advantage of her unwillingness to speak up and she eventually ended her marriage at the age of forty-five.

As she looks back on her life leading up to the age of forty-five, she regrettably felt as if she had so many gifts her shyness kept her from giving. She felt there was so much more living she could have done by igniting her unique gifts and talents.

She allowed her shyness to box her in from saying yes to so much of life. *"Wouldn't it be wonderful if I could rewind time and change that part of my adult life to experience the freedom I have today,"* she thought to herself.

I asked Jane what she would say to her younger self, given the chance. She paused and responded with: *"I would tell her that she is everything that she needs to be. She is talented, gifted, warm and loving and that the world needs her gifts."*

~ Inspired Insights ~
INFLUENCERS LIVE BIG QUESTIONS

Influencers contemplate these deeper questions:
What do you need to release? What energy no longer serves you?
What do you need to embrace to move your life in the direction you intend to go?

Jane attempted to find herself in her second marriage that lasted twenty-one years. Within this longer and more arduous marriage, she found it increasingly difficult to have a voice in the presence of her dominant husband. He refused to let her work.

It was finally through this turbulent experience that Jane's true voice emerged. *"At the age of forty-five I finally arrived at my tipping point. I was no longer prepared to live this way and was ready to start my new life, so I decided to leave the marriage."* Soon after the divorce, a special friend who was an author recommended that she enrol in a personal growth and development course in *Sandpoint Idaho. "I respected and trusted his insights. He encouraged me to learn how to speak as proficiently as I could write."*

Jane knew she could no longer hide in the shadows. She needed to step into the light and learn how to command her voice in the presence of others. Her confidence grew over the next four years while undertaking personal development courses under the direction of life coach: *Kendrick Mercer. "I spent a lot of time, energy and money but it was all worth it! This journey changed my life!"* she enthusiastically shared.

She learned to *love* who she was and how to get outside of herself and live with a greater sense of curiosity for other people.

To this day she fights to rise above the engrained shyness that she feels exists deep within her. She is able to recognize the natural-born tendency to retreat into the shadows and now catches herself before it happens. *"I have always been highly resilient. Despite not having a lot of work experience at the age of forty-five...I never felt more free in my life."*

I admire Jane's courage to finally stand up for herself and break away from the emotional bondage she experienced all those years.

~ Inspired Insights ~
INFLUENCERS DESIGN THEIR LIVES

We are the designers of our lives.
We shape and define our own reality through belief, faith and inspired action.

She was finally free to *design* her new life on her terms. Jane became an interior designer at the young age of forty-five. She was ready to define herself by creating the life of her dreams. She always had an eye and an appreciation for style and beautiful things. She was exposed to renovating a number of homes and had a natural feel for how spaces flowed. With a clear picture of the distant horizon, she created her own design business that thrived for eleven years.

The successful businesswoman that lay dormant for more than half of her life, finally burst into a ball of fiery success. The commitment to personal development years ago created a strong foundation. It helped her ultimately find her voice and her courage to succeed.

When she decided to go within, she discovered a plethora of untapped talents and gifts waiting to be unleashed. *Pandora's Box* was finally cracked open and the light filled her heart and lit up her soul. She was unstoppable in her interior design business. She embraced the power of communication and relished at connecting with her new clients. Her reputation in designing large assisted living facilities, expanded throughout the state. *"It became a real joy for me to have command for who I was and what I was able to do. My new mindset helped me thrive in these large corporate settings."*

She loved having her own money and the power to choose and create her own freedom. This passion now fuels her new-found purpose in helping women carve out a new sense of financial independence.

Even though they had their own challenges communicating, she admires her mother as being one of her greatest influencers. *"She taught me that I could do anything that I put my mind to."* Her mother instilled a strong work ethic in her.

Jane admired how her mother lovingly stayed up until 2:00am sewing all of her school clothes even after working a full day. *"It wasn't that we couldn't afford to buy clothes. My mother chose to make all of my outfits as an act of love."*

Her mother even inspired Jane to work at six years of age in the fields, picking berries and vegetables so she could have her own money. Jane's desire for independence inspired her to leave the fields and begin working in her father's optometry clinic at the age of twelve. *"I learned at an early age how to work in a professional setting."*

Kendrick Mercer influenced Jane to master the art of communication. Her Aunt Norma who recently died at the age of ninety-two, inspired her to grab a hold of life and live it to the fullest. *"My Aunt Norma was such a hoot and the antithesis of what I had ever been. I just loved being around her joyous and playful energy."*

~ Inspired Insights ~
INFLUENCERS EMBRACE OTHERS

Surround yourself with people that see the greatness within you. Embrace their joyous energy and receive their gifts as they reach out and inspire you to shine.

Jane defines an influencer as someone who inspires you to see something in a different way. They pull back the curtain and help you reveal the greatness within. This beauty is often concealed from us. *"Influencers have a belief that is so powerful that you can borrow it until you actually believe and feel it yourself."*

Influencers like her Aunt Norma are larger than life. Their contagious passion washes over others like a crashing ocean wave. You can't help getting swept up in their energy.

Jane eventually came to the belief that life was no longer just about her but rather serving other people. It became about receiving their gifts of *influence* and then asking what she could do for them.

"I feel it deep in my core as if I've arrived at a point in my life where I'm truly fulfilled serving others, from all walks of life." She believes in her purpose to contribute to the richness of others people's lives.

~ Inspired Insights ~
INFLUENCERS SHARE THEIR JOY

Influencers experience tremendous joy when giving to others.
They believe in an energy of connection. They celebrate their gifts by giving them away.

She sees herself as someone who gives value back to other people regardless of their status in society. She surrounds herself with like-minded people that thrive on the energy of giving. Whether connecting with her design clients or leading others in her current international business, she strives to give back value to everyone she comes in contact with.

Her greatest growth as a leader stems from her deeper curiosity in people. She thrives on face-to-face and heart-to-heart contact in this *'connection age.'* *"People are fascinating and they love to talk about themselves."*

Jane's transformation from an introvert into a global leader has had a significant positive and lasting impact on her family; especially her two daughters; Libby and Holly. *"Aside from my daughters feeling very proud of who their mother has become, they know that I'm always there to catch them if they fall and to help them grow."*

Her wish for others is to uncover how beautiful and talented they are. She believes that if people really love who they are at their core, then the emotions of anger, jealousy and hate would cease to exist in our world.

Throughout all of her trials and tribulations she chose to lead with love. *"I have made love for others my daily mantra. Regardless if someone cuts me off or hurts me in some way, I choose to love everyone and accept them where they are. When you stand in the light of love no one can come against you."*

One of her favourite quotes from her mentor *David Byrd* written on her office wall reads: *"We are all perfect...yet incomplete."* This is the energy of love that Jane desires to see live on. *"God created us perfectly but we're not finished. This inspires me to give other people grace."*

~ Inspired Insights ~
INFLUENCERS CHOOSE LOVE OVER FEAR

Fear cannot co-exist in a mind that is filled with love.
Love everyone and everything that shows up in your beautiful life.

She has learned to embrace every unfolding in her life as having a purpose. She welcomes change as a catalyst for her greatest growth. Regardless of where her path takes her in the next ten years, she is open to believing that she is a better person today than she was a year ago.

Jane shared with me her top tips for influencing others:

- Choose to *love* other people where they are.
- Get *curious* about other people. It opens up their heart to receiving your gifts.
- Be *grounded* in who you really are. Know yourself.
- Don't give credence to what other people think of you. If you're doing the right thing just remember we are *all* a work in progress.
- In order to *grow* you must make mistakes and fail forward.

When I asked Jane what her five grandchildren would say about the influence she had on them she responded; *"My grandsons would say I was rock solid and that I loved them to their core. My granddaughters would say I was a role model that taught them to be grounded, strong, loving and to never settle for just an average life."*

Jane learned to design a new *inner-world* by embracing the uniqueness of others. She helped create a world filled with joy, love and an appreciation for one another's gifts. Her legacy will be felt by generations as a loving leader who not only found her booming voice but also inspired others to find and *love* theirs.

"IF YOU HAVE NEVER FALLEN YOU HAVE NEVER CHALLENGED YOUR POTENTIAL."

~ Gerry Visca

"BE FOOLISH! IT'S A FAR MORE INTERESTING WAY TO LIVE!"

~ Gerry Visca

Photography by: Dan Voyer

9. Lisa McLellan

Understand Yourself

"I exist for the truth of unconditional love." ~ Lisa McLellan

*L*isa McLellan grew up with privilege in an idyllic rural environment in a loving family. On her father's side existed a long line of physicians and nurses. On her Mother's, the head of the Dutch Cavalry and the Governor General of Java, sitting under a gold umbrella held by Indonesian servants. Privilege can have its drawbacks. And in her case the distancing belief that you are better than others lead her on a long journey that shaped her life to come.

Around the age of fifteen, Lisa awoke to the truth that she was sheltered from reality, living in her beautiful 'glass tower'. This awareness of the duality of *reality* that existed in the world around her, created a growing sense of unease and deeper curiosity within her.

"I wondered what it would be like to face the 'truth' of real hardship and poverty. It was the truth that drove me." What troubled her the most was the feeling that the charmed life she was living...was an illusion.

"I wanted to understand the truth of what people had to go through in life." She sensed that her 'ivory tower' protected her from

realizing the deeper truth of her heart and feeling what human suffering really meant. *"I recall asking my mother at around ten years old if we could have a picnic down by the pool and pretend we were poor,"* she added with a laugh.

~ Inspired Insights ~
INFLUENCERS REMAIN CURIOUS

Influencers are deeply curious about the world around them and their role in shaping it. Their thirst for knowledge never stops.

Her parents viewed her as rebellious. Lisa didn't see it that way. She saw herself as someone who was following her heart and her inner voice. Her curiosity for understanding the truth inspired her to do things *differently* than what was expected of her.

In the 80's, around the time she moved away from home to attend university, she shaved half her head and began wearing clothes from the *Salvation Army.* As the oldest child, her parents were appalled.

"I love my parents deeply, but at the time they didn't feel comfortable with me stepping outside the box, breaking the rules and wanting to change the world. My mom wanted me to marry a rich man and follow the status quo."

INFLUENCERS DEFY THE SYSTEM

Influencers don't follow the status quo.
They take pleasure in colouring outside the lines. They choose to see the world from a different lens.

Lisa's heart ached to express itself by living her truth. She felt that her true nature was being crushed under the weight of having to live the lie of being better than others. She had to conceal her true emotions and curiosity in the shadows. She was perplexed that her drive to understand the world could be so disruptive to others.

Her curiosity evolved into feeling a sense of distrust at how *cold* the mind can be. She knew herself to be a warm, loving and kind person. This split was so painful. She struggled with the dichotomy to release her mind so she could live with her heart.

"My incessant need to love and care for others must have been a gene that I inherited from my father's side of the family."

The answers to her deeper curiosity came to her through the teachings of *Somatic Movement*. *"I'm a kinaesthetic learner. I've always loved to move. I love anything that has to do with using my body for expression. It's where I found my freedom."* Around the age of twenty Lisa attended a summer program at *Connecticut's Wesleyan University* learning the fundamentals of body-mind integration, a powerful movement in the 80's. *"This is where I learned about the language of the body and how it reflects and responds to what you feel and think. I grasped a deeper appreciation in how to work with the body in order to help people understand themselves."*

Somatic Movement became the 'key' towards understanding how to move people towards wholeness. Her development in this field for the past thirty years helped her unlock the mystery of wholeness; the balance between her thinking and the mind of her heart.

Through the practice of embodied movement, she learned to release years of pent up feelings and judgments based on what she was taught and what she 'should do' in the eyes of society. *"I was able to confront these inner challenges and make friends with them as a result of being able to move them through my body."*

~ Inspired Insights ~
INFLUENCERS BECOME THE CHANGE THEY SEEK

Influencers go within to gain a deeper understanding of who they are and the change they wish to see in the world.

Lisa had a long-held desire to be free from the shackles of what society deemed *right* and *normal*. She craved a life of freedom of being. *"For years I battled with my father who was a physician as to the merits of preventive approaches versus medical science. I became angry and frustrated. Eventually we agreed to disagree. I learned intellectual rigour from him for which I am grateful. He came to my classes, felt the benefits and enjoyed watching me teach. The disagreement never interfered with the love we had for each other,"* she recounted.

This dichotomy once again found its way into her professional career. On the one side, was her father who is a strong and superior thinking physician who lived through scientific results (mind). While on the other, she longed to embrace a more preventive and holistic approach (body/heart).

She felt as if she was imprisoned in a cultural box and that the hidden agenda of mental snobbery was holding her back. *"My mind made me self conscious, insecure and doubtful of who I was. I suffered through the fear of expressing myself."* She longed to breakout of the box to reveal her real self. Perseverance in the practice of body-mind integration helped her find balance with both the scientific mind and her heart.

Today at the young age of fifty-seven she longs to help people free themselves so they can move through their authentic self. *"After forty-two years of experience working with infants right up to ninety-six year old adults, I see a common theme in everyone; a desire for joy and total inner freedom."*

She has guided and empowered people from all walks of life including: professional dancers and artists; people with mental health challenges; ex drug addicts; neglected children and everyday people from various levels of education.

"With a gentle and loving approach I help people release the energy that is holding them back. I'm passionate about empowering people to love themselves so they can fulfill their natural potential."

~ Inspired Insights ~
INFLUENCERS CREATE A RIPPLE OF LOVE

Influencers lead with love.

They embrace their unique gifts by helping others love themselves.

For the past sixteen years, Lisa has focused her energy on the 'question of aging.' *"People are unaware of the dramatic impact the aging population will have on life as we know it. My intention is to guide with my compassion and real-life experience to spark greater awareness for this global impact and to get people stepping up to the plate."* Her research reveals that by 2050 there will be five people sixty-five and over for every one person fifteen to sixty-four. These projections are staggering and have never existed before in our history.

By the time Lisa turned forty, she was living in the *Laurentian Mountains* raising her ten year old son. As a single mom with no assistance, she was easily working seventy to eighty hours per week running a non-profit community arts organization focused on cultivating creativity in the schools. *"I realized five years into it that I didn't even have time for my own child! I knew things had to change,"* she recounted.

A significant part of her *being* cannot accept what is *untrue.* It's this vision and energy that propelled her through life regardless of the challenges she faced. Around the age of forty, she chose to give up her exhausting role with the non-profit organization and *shift* her career as a personal trainer specializing in the fifty *plus* demographic.

What Lisa knew for certain was her passion for *transformation through movement.*

Despite the naysayers, she diligently carved out a new market in her community using the skills she had learned integrating somatic movement, transformation and free expression in institutions such as schools.

At the time, fitness centres didn't offer specialized classes for this aging demographic. With Lisa's influence she managed to successfully pull together and personally enrol a group of older people to experience the first ever in her community, a fifty *plus* fitness/well being class.

~ Inspired Insights ~
INFLUENCERS GENERATE MOMENTUM

Influencers don't wait for others to drive the change they are seeking to create in the world. They take action and create powerful momentum.

Lisa's father inspired in her a 'pioneering spirit'. His energy gave her the courage to go out and pursue the life she wanted. *"He is a joyful and creative spirit. He always taught me that there was a solution for every problem."*

At the age of fifty-seven her father retired from the medical world ironically as a result of being *disenchanted* with the system. Together with Lisa's mother, they sailed the *Caribbean* six months of the year for the next twelve years. Her father inspired her to think *outside the box* while her mother taught her the rules *of the box.*

The influencers that shaped her way of being in the fitness industry were *Somatic Movement* teachers who carried forward ground breaking *Irmgard Bartenieff Fundamentals, Rudolph Laban Effort/Shape and Bonnie Bainbridge Cohen Body-Mind Centering.*

"These teachers gave me the tools and techniques that I needed to take my natural talents and bring them forth into the world. They helped me connect to my personal power."

Lisa has since adopted these earlier techniques and combining them with her training in Modern Dance innovated her unique approach that she employs in her *Age Smart Fitness Academy.*

She also studied *Tibetan Buddhism* from the age of twenty-five to thirty where she learned the art of *Maitri* (*Sanskrit* for loving kindness) and meditation. *"These Buddhist teachings had a profound influence on how I use my mind. They gave me the integrative tools to balance my body and mind, to free myself and shape the way I serve others today as a guide and trainer."*

~ Inspired Insights ~
INFLUENCERS LEAD KNOWING WHY

Influencers live through the philosophy that when the student is ready the teacher will appear. They surrender their need to know HOW and trust that their deeper WHY will ignite the WAY.

Lisa embraced the following actions and thinking along her journey of influence:

- *Creating* a simple and holistic approach to exercise as well being.

- *Developing* body awareness.
- *Embracing* a positive mindset.
- *Experiencing* new levels of joy.

"Around the year two thousand when the medical system in Canada and Quebec was beginning to fall apart, it occurred to me that I was transforming older people into more energetic and healthier individuals. They started experiencing less pain and having a positive outlook on life."

Through a simple approach to movement and exercise, Lisa began inspiring a new light of hope and vitality within the aging population of her community. *"They had more energy! They were happier and empowered with more knowledge and resources. Rather than be a drain on society due to ill health they were contributing their wisdom, expertise and resources to the community."*

Through this vibrant knowledge base, she created a thriving network and ripple effect that began influencing a stronger and more vibrant foundation within her local community.

Like most influencers, the *seed of the idea* entered her consciousness many years ago. She was becoming the change she was seeking in others by attracting the teachers and the way as a result of igniting her deeper, driving why.

She continues to conduct and share extensive and alarming research about the burden the aging population is going to exert on our fragile world; she shared with me how it is an inevitable fact that will impact us all. But also how it is an amazing opportunity to transform the way we view aging and the crucial role an older population will play in a changed world.

Lisa has a powerful intention to help *Boomers* and seniors take 100% responsibility for their personal health and mindset with joy. *"What I have come to learn is that while 'being healthy' is essential it's no longer enough to solve this inevitable global crisis. People are now living far into their nineties. Simply trying to retire, sit back and coast along is no longer working,"* she added with a deep sense of concern.

She shared how we are *now* facing a new reality where people are working long past the age of sixty-five and rethinking the idea of retirement. Lisa is focused on *shifting* this paradigm. She is building awareness for the need to *reinvent* this older way of thinking about age, retirement and meaningful living.

"We need new strategies and new levels of thinking to prepare and address this global phenomenon. The only reason someone wants to retire is their work is exhausting them and not fulfilling their desired way of life!"

Her passion as an *influencer of change* resides in addressing the fitness and the well being side of this issue by influencing positive movement into our aging population. Lisa is helping people face the fear of change and developing new and inspirational ways to live out the best years of their lives.

She believes that everyday people can become people of influence. *"A person of influence is a role model that is not above you but rather one that walks along side you. They inspire a new sense of belief that we too can walk in those shoes."*

Influencers guide others with the energy of inclusion encouraging others to step along side them in order to bring out the best in everyone.

~ Inspired Insights ~
INFLUENCERS LIVE THROUGH POSSIBILITY

Inside each one of us lives a power and an ability to influence positive change in the world. Influencers rise above challenges. Their minds soar into the skies of possibility, yet their hearts beat alongside everyone.

Influencers magnetically stand out from the crowd by communicating their message with love, inspiration and authenticity. Their willingness to look foolish and fail forward inspires everyday people to take the first step towards driving change in their lives.

"Influencers are people that we love and admire. They instil new levels of belief and possibility within us," she shared.

Through all of Lisa's hard work and determination, she is influencing a new shift in mindset about how we view and treat an aging humanity. She has chosen a challenging path to live out her deeper, driving why. These choices to influence change have made her stronger.

Women Inspiring Change

"Despite embracing an arduous path, I have become more resourceful, stronger and confident. In order to realize greater levels of awareness, I need to strengthen collaboration with other global influencers. I know that I cannot do this alone."

Her perseverance is creating a foundation for freedom that will be felt within generations that follow. Her authenticity will be absorbed into people's hearts like a shining light illuminating the way for others to carry on. She is influencing change by standing tall and declaring her intention with the energy of confidence and charming grace.

"People are so surprised that I am fifty-seven years of age. I believe you can age but not feel old. Imagine a world where we age yet we feel more active, free, alive and full of passion!"

Lisa is shifting the world's perception of 'growing old' by inspiring a new mindset of invigorating possibility. *"Growing old no longer needs to be seen as losing one's vitality but rather, a celebration of the next exciting chapter of our lives. Older is the New Cool."*

~ Inspired Insights ~
INFLUENCERS FOCUS ON THE BIGGER PICTURE

Influencers don't look for the easiest path to inspire change.
They live with a deeper sense of belief that the bigger picture of their lives will unfold.

She has a strong intention for driving new levels of awareness and change into: systems and global policies, our workplace and in our daily lives. *"To see this dream realized, I believe it's going to require a collective consciousness and desire from many different actors. We need strong corporate advocates to drive change within the workplace. When we all choose to roll up our sleeves we will influence a new mindset. We better start now."*

Lisa's approach to inspiring our aging population is one of ease and pleasure. *"Many older people simply lack the skills and knowledge towards moving their mind and body and creating new levels of energy,"* she adds.

She is creating a world that celebrates the gift of being alive. *"The first step regardless of age,"* she begins, *"Is that people start taking charge of their own health. We continually need new levels of energy to keep the passion and fires burning within our hearts and there are simple solutions for achieving this."*

She believes that we can all feel this greater sense of vitality coursing through our cells when we harness new levels of creativity, influence and inspiration.

She sees a changing world where people are now inspired to work into their seventies. *"There is an urgent need to shift the corporate paradigm with new levels of self-motivation. Perhaps we don't need to work five days a week in order to be more productive and give our best selves. It's about creating new levels of work-life balance that supports this changing model."*

She envisions innovative work places that seamlessly integrate meditation, relaxation and fitness spaces that elevate the human spirit, and cafeterias that provide its employees with healthy and nutritious foods. Multiple generations working seamlessly and harmoniously to get the best from one another.

She imagines a world where we honour our aging population with greater levels of respect, dignity and grace; a world where the continuity of *energy and vitality* are seen as the lifeblood for all humanity. This is the common thread that needs to carry through the various stages of our lives.

"The cost of sick people is astronomical. Our global economy will not be able to support this momentum of illness. With the aging population being the largest demographic ever in history we need proactive approaches to creating sustainable health."

~ Inspired Insights ~
INFLUENCERS HARNESS NEW LEVELS OF ENERGY

Influencers know that without higher levels of energy they cannot reach new levels. They condition their mind, body and spirit on a daily basis.

Lisa's wish for others is to live with *radiant health*. This is the outcome she wishes others to experience. She defines *radiant health* as an energy of vitality that emanates outward and ignites the light within others.

"That energy of light is: consciousness, the heart and unconditional love. It's the ultimate union of body and mind. When people experience radiant health as a way of being, they become inspired to mentor others through their unique gifts and transcend their knowledge."

She is creating *equanimity of spirit* that will benefit all of humanity. *"When this equanimity is infused within all layers of society we free the human mind and contribute to everyone's growth. We strengthen human relationships and interconnectivity. Inside each one of us is an ability to transcend our passion, purpose and wisdom."*

Lisa's top tips for influencing change are:

- *Walk your talk* authentically for the benefit of the world.
- *Be heard* by sharing your light and your unique gifts with others.
- *Lead* through an energy of empathy and compassion.
- *Make choices* that affect the wellbeing and sustainability of mother earth.
- *Be relatable.* Inspire others to be and do the same.
- *Focus* on helping people become successful. Make it about them.
- *Lead* yourself with passion, belief and persistence.

~ Inspired Insights ~
INFLUENCERS IGNITE HUMANITY

Influencers lead with their heart for the benefit of all humanity.

Their belief in their light radiates an outward energy that inspires others to take action.

Lisa is opening people's minds and influencing awareness for change with a sense of ease and flow. She is creating a legacy of positive change by taking up the torch and helping to lay the foundation for future generations. She is rolling up her sleeves with a joyous and positive energy connecting others one brick at a time.

Her energetic and proactive approach is helping to ease the transition of aging. She is disrupting the status quo and casting a light on an aging population. She is inspiring a world of *radiant health.*

She is not afraid of looking foolish, falling down or failing forward. She has a relentless belief towards influencing global change. Lisa allows her *inner impulse* to light the way and influence others around her to be and do the same. She walks alongside everyone as a collaborator of humanity.

Lisa McLellan is an influencer with a radiant heart.

"SURROUND YOURSELF WITH PEOPLE THAT WON'T ALLOW YOU TO PLAY SMALL."

~ Gerry Visca

10. Marsha Vanwynsberghe

Digging Deeper

"I exist to inspire others to see and believe in themselves."

~ Marsha Vanwynsberghe

*M*arsha was exposed to a number of challenges early in life. She attributes who she is today to her experiences and all of the difficult decisions that she never truly felt ready to make. When do we ever feel ready to make the hard decisions in life?

"I am who I am today because of everything that I have experienced. To be grateful for who I have become requires that I express gratitude for the good and the hard experiences that life presented to me." There are lessons everywhere if we choose to see them.

Her journey began at the tender age of twelve when she was a victim of assault from a group of boys in her school. This arduous experience impacted her deeply and influenced her to take 100% responsibility for her life. *"I'm stubborn to a fault in that I would do things my way and take life in my hands."*

Marsha's *decisiveness* surrounded her like a warm blanket of light for years. *"I was clear on what I wanted,"* she recounted. At the age of sixteen, a teacher in grade eleven sparked her curiosity for pursuing the field of *kinesiology*. This was her way of living with a sense of certainty. She knew from a young age what she wanted to experience and why.

She ended up marrying her high school sweetheart. *"I do not know where I would be without him. He brings out a part of me that I am beyond grateful for."* Prior to getting married, she was determined to become self-sufficient and fiercely independent.

~ Inspired Insights ~
INFLUENCERS REMEMBER WHY

Influencers are open to an energy of learning from an early age.
They listen to the whispers from the universe with the intent to understand.

She was exposed to leadership from an early age and was selected to attend a three-day leadership retreat around the age of twelve. *"This opportunity changed my life! It helped shape my outlook on taking 100% responsibility for the life I desired to create. I always knew there was somebody else I could learn from."*

She savoured learning and personal development and found herself open to inspiration from anywhere she could get it. She envisioned herself leading and influencing others with an open heart from an early age. *"I believed that I could make a difference in helping others. This belief led me to leading teams, collaborating and serving on my high school student council."*

A desire for learning and leadership was ingrained in her cellular DNA. She found herself craving and thirsting for more. Personal development continued to be an inspired way of being.

Every year, she found herself attending more events and surrounding herself with a wave of inspiring leadership experts.

~ Inspired Insights ~
INFLUENCERS CRAVE PERSONAL DEVELOPMENT

Influencers shape their desired reality by surrounding themselves with inspired learners. They crave new levels of personal development.

She entered her first public speaking contest at the age of ten. By sharing her words and voice, she intuitively knew she was meant to be a light for others. *"A lot of people approached me for my opinion and I believed in my ability to find the answer."*

The genesis of her driving purpose stemmed from shining a light on other people. *"I was filled up by looking for the potential in others,"* she adds.

These earlier life challenges taught her to persevere and face any obstacle head on. *"I've always felt that the answer lay deep within me. I just needed to slow down, trust in this inner knowing and learn how to extract it. My intuition has become a rock for me so I tend to listen with the intent to understand."*

She honours the whispers from her heart and soul. They have served her well in identifying the most direct path to take.

Marsha longed for simplicity, clarity and order. *"Because of being a Type A personality, one of my greatest challenges stem from* an incessant need to have the answer figured out ahead of time."

Today, she still craves a life of simplicity. She strives to take great pleasure in the smallest of things. *"I crave inner peace by carving out the time to fill my up soul through meditation, yoga and good nutrition."*

When she fills up her own cup through self-reflection, she overflows with a sense of certainty and clarity and is able to give more to others. *"The more that I take care of me, the more I handle the complexities of life and perform at new levels."*

Upon graduating from *kinesiology* she had a long-held desire of being a *problem solver.* Her expertise stemmed from *helping* people with extreme physical issues who have reached the end of their rope with no clear result in site.

"These are my absolute favourite people to work with. When they are ready I take them through a powerful journey of helping them get back to doing what they love."

This energy has successfully transcended into her coaching practice. Whether her clients are deeply held back from intense physical, personal or emotional issues, she is able to move them forward and help them create their desired outcomes.

Marsha loves helping people with the most challenging situations by being a light and guiding them out of the darkness. *"I'm not afraid to help people tackle the hard things in life. I savour the opportunity of digging deeper."*

~ Inspired Insights ~

INFLUENCERS INSPIRE MEANINGFUL OUTCOMES

Influencers gain knowledge for the benefit of others. They have a desire to help others create meaningful outcomes. They strive to serve others with their light and their unique gifts.

The severe challenges of substance abuse that appeared within Marsha's family six years ago resulted in her temporarily losing herself. She found herself facing an uncertain future and spiralling out of control. *"I didn't want to stay in that difficult space so I shifted from trying to 'fix the situation' to embracing personal development,"* she adds.

This *empowered* way of being became a powerful catalyst for embracing the learnings through personal development. She painfully realized that the only thing she could control was herself.

As she opened her heart and mind, she naturally gravitated towards inspiring people. *"It's only been in the past eighteen months that I can truly say I found myself again. Guided meditations were instrumental in strengthening my physical mind,"* she recounted. She continues to work on her mind on a consistent and daily basis.

She knew that the only thing she was able to control was the present moment. That is where she learned to strengthen herself. Through the persistent practice of guided meditation and yoga she let go of the negative energy of the past and her anxiety for the future.

These challenges influenced her to surround herself with only positive and uplifting people. *"I became extremely particular about who I surrounded myself with,"* she recalled.

~ Inspired Insights ~
INFLUENCERS DON'T WASTE TIME CHANGING OTHERS

Influencers don't waste their energy on things they cannot control. They strengthen their mind through personal development. When they internally change the way they look at things, that's when everything external changes.

Marsha's hard-working and diligent parents have been a huge source of influence to her in a number of ways. Her grandmother helped shape her character at a very young age. She helped Marsha embrace her independent nature. They remained very close into her final eighty-seventh year.

"She was the most beautiful and supportive non-judgmental person during the most turbulent times of my family's life. With her last breath she shared how proud she was of my husband and I, for how we handled such a difficult and ongoing situation. Speaking at her funeral two years ago sparked my current way of being and serving others."

Marsha is filled with gratitude for several teachers in her high school that influenced her that she could be and do anything. A series of close friends over the years, have helped her strengthen her belief systems. *"My loyal husband's unconditional belief and encouragement has had a profound impact on me. Not only does he remind me to have fun, he let's 'me be me' by allocating the space I need."*

She shared a powerful insight that rocked me to my core: *'Surrendering doesn't mean giving up!'* This deeper awareness inspired her to become a better role model for her children.

She embraced the following *actions* and new *thinking* during the difficult times she faced:

- She *learned* how to *trust* herself. (She doubted herself as a parent because she couldn't fix the problem).

- She *developed* the capacity to release the problem that wasn't hers to fix.

- She *learned* to surrender *control* and let go of the outcomes.

- She learned to manage her expectations and live in the present moment with gratitude.

- She *surrendered* her ego and reached out to everyone and turned over every rock for support.

- She *put on* her own oxygen mask and filled herself up in order to be in a position to fill up others.

- She *created* boundaries for her own safety and headspace through consistent and daily meditation, yoga, writing and personal development.

~ Inspired Insights ~
INFLUENCERS ELEVATE OTHERS

Influencers release the energy that no longer serves them.
They embrace actions and 'right thinking' that elevates all those around them.

Marsha defines an influencer as a *difference maker*. They are in tune with the energy of the world and aware of their role to help shape it. *"Influencers can see outside of themselves and believe that their everyday actions can be of service to others."*

Everyday people can be influencers but it requires a deeper realization that we all have *gifts* to share with the world. Influencers strive to ignite these unique abilities so they can confidently serve others through them.

"I believe that our greatest gifts are buried deeply within the challenges that we are meant to face day in and day out."

What separates influencers from others is there willingness to *uncover* and *ignite* these gifts during their darkest times. *"Influencers feel the fear and do it anyway. They see the bigger picture of the change they wish to create. They stand up, stand out and find their voice,"* she added.

~ Inspired Insights ~
INFLUENCERS DON'T WAIT FOR SOMEDAY

Influencers realize their time on this earth is limited. They don't wait for 'someday' to become the change they are seeking to inspire in others.

Marsha's belief in herself as an influencer *overflows* with abundance that she pours into other people's cups. *"When I was at my lowest point, I borrowed the belief from others until I was able to believe in myself. I truly accept that we all have this inner belief tucked deeply within ourselves and we just need to learn how to extract it."*

She is helping influence a judgment-free world through energy of kindness, acceptance and compassion.

Her wish for others is to become aware of their gifts and unbridled possibility that lives and breathes inside of us all. *"Most of us barely scratch the surface of what we are truly capable of achieving."*

She believes that for the necessary shifts to occur in our world, all of humanity will need to awaken and live through their *unique gifts. "I'm prepared to step into that life-altering space by helping others claim theirs. This is the beautiful energy that I envision rippling out into the world."*

~ Inspired Insights ~
INFLUENCERS SHIFT THE WORLD'S ENERGY

Influencers live with a deeper and more profound vision for humanity. They believe that through a collective consciousness we can elevate and shift the world's energy.

One of the ways that Marsha helps instil new levels of belief in others is by working closely with people to *strip away* all of the excuses and the things that don't matter. She *digs* into the root of the matter by helping people take 100% responsibility for the things that they can control. She then helps them create the daily habits to support positive change. *"All change comes from within."*

For change to occur people have to want to change and believe it's possible. *"To help people get to the root of it, sometimes it takes a stripping away of the excess garbage that is holding them back."*

Women Inspiring Change

~ Inspired Insights ~
INFLUENCERS RELEASE LIMITING BELIEFS

Influencers deconstruct their lives by shedding away their past limiting beliefs.
They influence their desired outcomes by taking 100% responsibility for being the
architect of their lives.

"When we are listening and stepping into what we truly want, then it doesn't matter what anyone else thinks about the changes you wish to experience in your life," she added.

Marsha shared that most people lack the *clarity* as a result of not knowing what they want. They allocate their energy to worrying what people think or comparing themselves to others. *"When we can help others become aware of their own thoughts we can help them work on developing new belief systems."*

The following are Marsha's top tips for strengthening your belief system:

- *Assume* 100% responsibility for where you are right now in your life with no judgment.
- *Strip away* the energy that no longer serves you.
- *Tap* into the bliss that truly makes you happy and fills you up.
- *Embrace* new levels of gratitude for being aware that you desire to make changes in your life.
- *Start* by making small incremental changes in your own life before being of service to others.

Marsha believes that her influence will impact generations to follow. She wants to be remembered as a *difference maker* who was unafraid to tackle the topics that nobody wanted to talk about.

She believes that she was put on this earth to make a profound difference. She found her voice when others needed to hear it the most. Her words helped light the way for people *buried* in the shadows by encouraging them to *climb* up into the light.

Marsha Vanwynsberghe is influencing people to dig deeper.

"LIFE ISN'T ABOUT ASKING HOW. LIFE IS ABOUT KNOWING WHY"

~ Gerry Visca

"WE ALL HAVE GIFTS TO SHARE, WHEN WE DO, THE WORLD CHANGES."

~ Gerry Visca

11. Chiara J-Megna

Creating Change That Matters

"I exist to inspire change in the world that truly matters."

~ Chiara J-Megna

*C*hiara J-Megna was born and raised in *Toronto*. She spent more than half of her childhood in Europe. Her father was a proud protestant of Hungarian descent and her mother was a passionate Irish catholic. These two opposing theologies collided in her earlier years often forcing her to choose a side.

She grew up in a very rigid and career-oriented environment. Her mother was a talented Canadian fashion designer and her father a determined engineer. Today, he is still the Chairman of *Bayshore Groups*, an international property acquisition, rehabilitation and redevelopment conglomerate.

Her childhood was unquestionably fruitful and derived much from her dad's pre dominant eastern influence. He exposed her to a wide array of sports like: rowing, skiing and the performing arts.

"My father was the dominant figure in our home. He enrolled us in prestigious academic environments to augment our future choices. We spoke four languages and I developed most of my discipline as a ballet dancer. When he travelled, my mom spoiled us with her fun and carefree energy," she recounted.

Her typical structured day as a child consisted of: rowing early in the morning, attending school, participating in extra curricular activities followed by evening reading in the bath tub. *"My parents were strong advocates of reading every night. A treat was being permitted to watch thirty minutes of television before we went to bed."*

The energy of independence was a strong influence in her early teens. Her parents were strong career-oriented people. Her mother spent a bulk of her time away from the family home pursuing her fashion career.

"The challenge was creating my own independence so my father decided to send me off to boarding school in Europe. After a year of learning I longed to return home and be with my family."

Even though she was grateful for her independence studying in Europe, she innately craved a deeper connection to her parents.

Chiara was a family-oriented person with a budding curiosity in her father's work. Even though she felt welcomed by her extended European family at sixteen years of age she chose to return to *Canada* and learn the ways of her father's business. *"Even though I didn't fully understand what I was getting involved in I loved what he did. I savoured the travel, the people and the humanitarian energy that my father exuded,"* she enthusiastically added.

She marvelled at the side of her father's philanthropic life. She enthusiastically participated in many galas and fund raising initiatives over the years to support the under privileged.

She chose to enrol in an art/sports school in Mississauga in order to reduce the need for extra curricular activities. This new found evening time allowed her to spend greater time learning her father's business.

~ Inspired Insights ~

INFLUENCERS ARE INSPIRED BY THEIR SURROUNDINGS

Our life choices are greatly shaped and influenced by the ring of our surroundings.
Choose to envelop yourself with people that ignite the energy of your true self.

She was never alone as a result of the vast array of friends and acquaintances that flowed through her father's company. Chiara naturally fostered the energy of independence as a result of being *entrusted* to find her own way. *"My mom even put me on a plane alone to Europe when I was only six years old to visit with my father who spent six months of the year growing his global business."*

At an early age she was inspired by her father's interconnection with people and the lifestyle he nurtured. *"My father instilled higher levels of discipline that helped me believe anything was possible. I often chose to sacrifice teenage experiences for a better future that enabled greater choices and rewards from my extra curricular activities."* She felt she missed out on cultivating high school friendships as a result of the opulent lifestyle her parents led.

"We continually moved homes and business locations so it was challenging nurturing friendships. It wasn't until I relocated back to Canada and attended high school in Mississauga where I created a stronger foundation of relationships that I still value to this day."

At the time she didn't share nor necessarily appreciate the myriad of extra curricular activities that her parents enrolled her in like: *piano, dance and flute lessons.* Little did she know that her discipline would ultimately crack-open her universe later on in her life.

"These earlier experiences influenced my independence. I eventually learned how to negotiate rewards by participating fully in these activities. I got to travel with my parents and spend more time in my father's plant."

Upon deeper reflection, Chiara felt she lived a fairytale lifestyle of both reward and reprimand. *"I remember feeling as if I had the perfect dad who exposed me to a life of abundance and discipline. I idolized my mother who came from a large family. She had the demeanour of an Irish princess. I felt like a black sheep in the shadows of my bounteous cousins from my mother's side of the family who all married into Irish families."*

Following high school she attended a Paramedic program in *Humber College* to widen her curiosity in *Kinesiology*. In high school she had primarily focused on engineering and drafting classes with the idea of following in her dad's footsteps.

"I loved using my creative faculties as a child drawing and creating at my drafting table. In high school I really wanted to pursue an architectural/engineering career. I originally enrolled at Ryerson Polytechnic Institute in Toronto but after seeing the students using computer assisted drawing programs I was discouraged to

attend. I was never a computer person and more passionate about using my hands."

Similar to her father, Chiara had a passion for helping people but little desire to sit behind a computer station all day so she chose to become a paramedic.

~ Inspired Insights ~
INFLUENCERS LIVE THEIR PASSION

We are born with innate gifts that are unique to each one of us.
When we live through our unique abilities we experience greater levels of
passion and purpose.

After embracing an occupation of working as a medic for a few years, she realized it would be challenging to stand out as a result of the influx of competition from young people entering the field. *"Despite my desire to work with my father, he was a strong advocate that my brother and I initially thrive in our own careers. My father never tabled the opportunity to work at his business until I earned my own way through life,"* she recalled.

She experienced challenges in forging a different career when her heart craved following in her father's footsteps. She eventually found the demands from the extensive night shifts physically and emotionally draining. She craved the discipline she came to appreciate as a child.

In 2001, she decided to return to school full time and become a police officer. She diligently attended school five days a week for

Women Inspiring Change

one full year. She graduated with honours as the highest honour role student in the history of the Police Foundations course. *"This was the most fulfilling experience of my life. The academic portion stimulated my mind and the intense physical training motivated my body. I fell in love with school again."*

As a result of her stellar academic standing she was stationed at the police headquarters in *Orillia, Ontario* where she met her husband, Robert.

~ Inspired Insights ~
INFLUENCERS STIMULATE THEIR MINDS

Influencers are students of life. Their thirst for knowledge and learning never stops.
They continually seek alternative ways to stimulate their mind and body.

She thrived in the police force for five years. However her mind was still set on working with her father. As a result of her flexible schedule at the police force she chose to spend time learning her father's business by immersing herself into the day-to-day activities.

"I played my cards very strategically with him. Even though he was concerned for my safety working as a police officer, he was pleased that I chose a career that strengthened my discipline and invigorated my mind and body," she added.

The previous years working on the front line as a paramedic and police officer opened her eyes to our human nature. Unlike the fairly tale world she grew up in she was now exposed to all types of ominous behaviour.

This experience strengthened her overall disposition. It influenced a greater appreciation of the many social layers that exists in our world. This realization helped her develop a sense of empathy for less fortunate people.

"This exposure to varying mindsets influenced me to be a better manager, stronger mother and a more respectful child." These deeper realizations even helped heal past wounds by looking at people in her life through a different lens.

"I am more forgiving of others and my relationship with my mother has grown stronger as a result. She was a great friend to me growing up but...not a great mother," she recalled.

Working in Orillia as a police officer, she chose to live her life with passion minute-by-minute. She was present and content with the life she was creating. Her proficient upbringing shaped a mindset of unbridled possibility.

She believed she could achieve anything she set her mind too. *"Unlike many people that live by setting endless future goals, I was raised to live in the passion of the moment."*

Today at the young age of forty she longs for a deeper understanding of her driving purpose and the hidden meaning as to *why she exists.* She has a long-held desire to connect the dots and bridge the gap from all of her extraordinary past accomplishments.

"I'm searching for greater clarity as to where all of this multi-generational hard work is leading to. I believe there is something

bigger on the horizon." She is on a mission to discern the deeper feeling behind her life and that it all mattered.

~ Inspired Insights ~

INFLUENCERS IGNITE THEIR DEEPER, DRIVING WHY

The greatest gift we can ever offer a fellow human being is to uncover the answer to the only question that truly matters: **Why do I exist?**

To this day she credits 50% of the success she experiences managing her father's global business, *Bayshore Groups* to her Eastern Italian husband Robert. When she first met him, she was attracted to the same engineering persona that existed in her father. *"It was very easy blending our families together as a result of the synergies that existed. We are both strong-headed and forward-thinking Sagittarians with similar energy levels and family values."*

203

One of the challenges they both face stems from their childhood conditioning to achieve more. *"Robert and I were both raised by very hardworking fathers. Instead of being content with maintaining the business my father created, we've adopted a risk-taking mindset that bigger is better."*

She admired her father's ability with being content with a business that earned hundreds of thousands of dollars versus the relentless pursuit towards building a multi-million dollar enterprise.

Chiara strives to face the energy of this growing dichotomy head on. *"This relentless desire inherent in our personalities to build an empire contributed to increased stress levels in our day-to-day lives,"* she openly shared.

Her father had a desire that family be involved with ongoing leadership in the company he founded. Since Chiara and her husband have taken over day-to-day operations they have experienced exponential growth.

Global *stability* continues to surface as one of Chiara's greatest challenges. *"Living in ten countries and working in more than thirty, I've witnessed social, political and economical shifts at all levels. It's not the same world that I grew up in."*

She shares how people's growing lack of empathy towards one another has created tremendous fear. She remembers a simpler time when her father could visit a *General Motors* plant and share a coffee over an inspiring conversation with the president.

"Today, the opportunity for this kind of personal and human connection is overshadowed by political hierarchy. I believe that future generations of our company will face even greater challenges in creating stability in how we run and manage our global business."

She is determined and passionate to infuse a stronger sense of wisdom and stability within the company enabling future generations to thrive.

~ Inspired Insights ~
INFLUENCERS BUILD LEGACIES

Influencers don't think about themselves.

Their selfless and outbound energy inspires future generations to carry the torch.

Women Inspiring Change

Her husband Robert is an instrumental influence as a partner and mentor in their company and loving husband and father in her life. *"I couldn't have found a more suitable partner who shares the same characteristics and mannerisms than Robert. I am so lucky in that regard. The dynamism of our energy flows very well together in all aspects of our lives."*

Despite being fifteen years apart in age it doesn't stop them from working and playing harder together. Growing up Chiara shared the difficulty in finding common ground with people her own age. She enjoyed the richness of life that her parents exposed her to. Attracting a mature man like Robert into her life was a perfect match.

As a young mom Chiara's friend Laura served as a strong support mechanism. *"She influenced me to create a thicker skin. She helped me strike a balance between motherhood and creating an empire with my husband. I often felt torn between these polarizing energies. To this day she is an angel sitting atop my shoulder."*

Her compassionate influencers exude a strong and calming rationalism in her life. It's these defining characteristics of influencers that Chiara feels is missing in her own persona. With her growing maturing wisdom she will become an "influencer" herself.

~ Inspired Insights ~
INFLUENCERS RISE ABOVE THEIR CURRENT CIRCUMSTANCES

Unlike most reactionary people, influencers think proactively.

They are not defined by their current circumstances.

"My friend Laura has a unique way in cooling down my Irish sensibility and helping me rationalize the bigger picture of a challenging situation. Her loving energy helps me focus on the smaller things in life that truly matter."

Listening to Chiara's heart, I believe she is influencing a new generation of inspired leadership. *"They help me change the way I look at a situation and my often unrealistic expectation of others."*

Despite her upbringing that anyone can do anything, she shared how her acceptance of others is her greatest opportunity for personal growth.

~ Inspired Insights ~
INFLUENCERS CHANGE THEMSELVES

"When you change the way you look at things - the things you look at change."

~ Dr. Wayne Dyer

The following represent Chiara's top actions for influencing change in one's life:

- *Create* greater levels of balance in all areas of your personal and professional life.
- *Stimulate* and condition your physical and mental well being. Training as an amateur boxer has sparked a deeper connection to her physical self that she lost over the years.
- *Ignite* your spiritual energy by going inward and allocating energy towards finding your deeper 'why'.

Coaching with me on her deeper, driving *"why"* over the past year, Chiara has uncovered the realization that she *exists to inspire change in the world that matters.* With this new-found awareness she asks herself everyday: **What is the change that matters?** She is inspiring others around her to define the change that matters most in their lives.

~ Inspired Insights ~
INFLUENCERS BECOME WHAT THEY SEEK

The most direct path to igniting your deeper purpose is to become the very thing you are seeking. The direct path to your higher self is to be what you seek.

Raising three of her own children and adopting three other children has been a rewarding and diverse experience in her life. She allocates tremendous thought towards uncovering which generation will be inspired to carry the torch. *"I am so proud of all of my children and the paths they have started to navigate but this question of legacy is still a grey area for me,"* she openly shared.

Chiara has a desire to be remembered as a woman that created an inspired life *her way* and on her terms. *"Whether the opinionated people around me like it or not, I lived the life I craved to live. How can I expect my kids to be any different from my influence?"*

She strives to forge a sense of generational stability while simultaneously living with the energy of radical acceptance. This is the dichotomy she faces in her fast-changing world. *"On one front I find myself heading out to the Dominican in the middle of closing a multi-million dollar deal. On the other...I spend hours creating strategic models to best carry this legacy into the future."*

Like most influential leaders; it's these dichotomies that fuels a richer blend to their lives. She has a strong intention of injecting *stability* into their expanding global business while maintaining a *radical spirit* in her personal life.

With every block and jab she breaks down the walls that pinned her spirit down as a young girl. Every right hook opens up a greater sense of inner freedom she is seeking.

Little did she know that the dichotomy that existed while growing up in her family life is now playing full out in her personal and professional life. The stability and discipline that her father engrained dances into the way she manages and expands her global business.

The freedom of spirit that she resisted in her mom now rages inside of her like a charging athlete. Speaking with Chiara I suddenly transform from an inspired author to the *why guy* and enthusiastically shouted out her new forward-thinking mantra: *Radical Stability.* She laughingly responded: *"I love it. Now I need to allocate the same amount of energy to living this deeper why that I pour into the other areas of my life."*

~ Inspired Insights ~
INFLUENCERS LIVE WITH ACCEPTANCE

What you resist persists. Acceptance is peace.

She feels an overwhelming sense of accomplishment in the professional career she has cultivated. She believes in the legacy she is *knocking out* for future generations. Her heart now craves a deeper sense of personal fulfilment in living the answer to the only question that matters; *Why am I here?*

Chiara leads with a philanthropic spirit. Her father led with an open door policy and often gave selflessly to others. This energy of inspiring change that matters continues to permeate her way of being in the world and how she clinches global frontiers.

She shared how in the earlier days of *Bayshore Groups* they took a reactive approach and donated to various causes on an as requested basis. Today, Chiara has narrowed her focus on supporting disadvantaged youth through her passion for boxing.

"I love kids. They are our future. It's the stability for them that we are focused on creating. Boxing has ignited my physical well being. As a child I wasn't allowed to savour this forbidden fruit. Today, I am playing the sport full out!"

This combination of giving to the next generation through physical activity feeds her soul. Chiara recently participated in her first amateur boxing match. Little did she know that this event would test her physical and mental capacity at whole new levels. Her father sat in the audience with his back turned away from the boxing ring. He couldn't stand watching his precious daughter endure this form of pain. *"As soon as I finished the match, I ran over and embraced him."*

209

Chiara was no stranger to *taking hits*. She gave birth to three children and adopted three others, and learned to build a thriving multi-million dollar corporation. Despite facing the trials and tribulations of her incredulous life this boxing experience was by far the hardest thing she ever endured.

~ Inspired Insights ~
INFLUENCERS SEE CHANGE AS GROWTH

Influencers push beyond the pain to create their desired way of being in the world.
They recognize that comfort suppresses their passion for the soul.
They look for ways to invite creative disruption into their lives.

Her wish for others is to take initiative and gain a deeper understanding of the complexities of our world. She would love for others to experience the universal beauty that she savoured as a young girl.

"I would love to see people expand their mind and appreciation of the multi-cultural diversities that exists throughout our planet. It saddens me that people in our local community of St. Catharines haven't even crossed the border into the USA. It's about influencing our children to focus on what truly matters in life."

Her wish for parents is to unveil our youth to the richness and diversity that exists within other cultures. *"For people to grow beyond their comfort zones and understand others they need to immerse themselves into unfamiliar surroundings."*

She relishes in meeting and interacting with hospitality staff all over the world. There is no hierarchy in her appreciation for fellow

Women Inspiring Change

human beings. She strikes up inspiring conversations with everyone she meets and listens with the intent to understand the diversity in other cultures.

"These experiences have shaped my life and my way of focusing on creating the change that matters. They have created a new lens from which to accept others."

The following summarizes Chiara's top tips for becoming a person of influence:

- *Life isn't about showing off it's about showing up.*
- *Avoid any debt that doesn't pay you and keeps you from living a life of passion and purpose. Get your money to do your heavy lifting.*
- *Seek out a millionaire mentor.*
- *Strive to create a sense of balance with your physical and mental health.*

"I believe in my ability to manifest any change in my life that matters." She has a desire to transcend her feisty and winning spirit into her children's hearts and influence *radical stability* across future generations. She wants her children to get off the ropes and ignite the flame that burns inside their hearts.

She has lived a full and selfless life. At the young age of forty, she is pushing herself to whole new levels. For the first time in her brilliant life, she is igniting the passion and purpose that feeds her soul.

Chiara J-Megna is a rare gem thriving in a fragmented world. She is influencing universal change that matters. Her compassion for others inspires us all to lace up our gloves and join the fight for humanity. She was raised as a student of life but today she is a teacher put on this earth to guide those around her through the energy of *radical acceptance.*

She is creating change that matters in her one precious life the only way she knows how...Chiara's way.

"**WRITE...**
as though it was your last word.

DREAM...
as though you were a child.

PERFORM...
as though the world was your stage. "

~ Gerry Visca

My story is your story

Imagine a World with 11,000 New Influencers

THE 11:11 PROJECT

*"We exist to elevate the energy of our world by inspiring One Million Whys. A world elevated by Why begins to create a new ROI for the world...where we exist to **R**each **O**ut and **I**nspire Others. This is a world inspired..."* ~ Gerry Visca and Angela Kontgen

*T*he great truth about life is that we are all *Influencers. Ghandi* called this *Influence*, a *Truth Force*; a *Love Force*...our *Soul Force*. The essence of *Influence* has little to do with position or power; rather *Influence* is an energy that emanates outward as we reconnect to the truth of who we really are and why we exist.

From this state we inspire this energy in others around us and a ripple is created as the world around us wakes up to their own inspired *Influence*...together we begin to shift the trajectory of our world and the destiny of humankind. Our world needs that now. Our world needs this kind of *Influence*…

This is the energy and spirit of this book that you hold in your hands. It's about everyday people doing the work to get clear on *why they are here*, taking action and stepping into their *Influence*. They are doing so not from a pedestal or place of 'having figured it all out' - rather they are stepping into their lives to influence others to do the same and to inspire the energy of *Influence* in others around them.

This book has been brought into existence to inspire 11,000 new *Influencers* in our world. It does not exist to become an *Amazon* best seller, in a day - who cares? And does that really make a difference in the world? We will inspire 11,000 new *Influencers* by connecting heart-to-heart and through the power of 11:11.

It begins with these women, sharing their story of influence and reaching out to inspire the influence in *eleven* people in their lives. Then the magic continues as each of these *eleven* reaches out to inspire *eleven* more. The stone has been cast and the *Ripple of Influence* now emanates out into our world. 11:11 is a wake up call - a call to wake up now and influence change in our world

Our Mission

Our mission with the *Influence Project* is to lay a foundation of greater meaning and purpose in the world and to ignite the *Influence* in each of us, one heart at a time and with the power of *eleven* together moving forward each taking on the mission to inspire

Women Inspiring Change

and ignite the *Influence* in another *eleven*. Each individual can serve humanity as a messenger of *Influence*.

How can you get involved? Create your tribe of influence; your tribe of *eleven.*

Decide today to step into your own positive *Influence* to help shift our world. Consider gathering eleven people in your universe and order them each a copy of this book. Create a *Tribe of Influence* and inspire one another to ignite the deeper, driving *Why* that lies within each of us. For the energy of *Influence* begins there and with you.

When you order *eleven books* you receive the gift of one-on-one *Why Time* and a group *Why session*, for your tribe, with *#whyguy* *Gerry Visca*. This is an inspiring phone/online session to help you and your tribe of *eleven* begin to dig deeper and begin to unveil the reason you are here. Inspire each person in your *tribe of influence* to carry this energy forward by encouraging them to order *eleven copies* of this book and continue the energy and the *Ripple of Influence* in the world. Imagine a world where *eleven thousand Influencers* know why they exist. This inspired energy will emanate outward and shift the trajectory of the world. Each one of us has been given the opportunity to light the flame of *Influence* in another. For Angela and I, we are ready and poised to light this candle.

Let's begin...

EMBRACE THE POSSIBILITY OF YOUR INFLUENCE.

"REACH OUT AND INFLUENCE OTHERS. IT'S A NEW ROI FOR THE WORLD."

~ Gerry Visca

INSPIRING TOOLS

Ignite your WHY

Worksheet
PASSION + PURPOSE = OUTCOME

PASSION

What excites me and makes me come alive?

_____

_____

What actions bring me the greatest joy?

_____

_____

PURPOSE

What service do I love giving away to others?

_____

_____

OUTCOME

What do I want to be remembered for?

_____

_____

_____

Scan this page to access this video training.

Visualization

Work Sheet

**Describe your ideal picture of what you want
your life to look like (WHY, WHAT, WHERE, WHEN, WHO)
Be as specific as possible.**

<u>WHY</u> DO YOU WANT IT?

_____

_____

_____

<u>WHAT</u> DO YOU WISH TO INFLUENCE?

_____

_____

_____

<u>WHERE</u> DO YOU WANT TO BE?

_____

_____

<u>WHO</u> DO YOU WANT TO INFLUENCE?

_____

_____

<u>WHEN</u> DO YOU WANT IT BY?

_____

_____

Women Inspiring Change

**Scan this page to access
this video training.**

Get Clear
Time Planner

Keep the energy alive by using this GET CLEAR© Planner. Get intentional and proactive about carving out time for your Influence, even if it is only an hour each week. If you don't schedule time to create, launch and live your vision, it won't come to life. This exercise will also bring awareness to how little time you are presently allocating to your dreams. Use the weekly section, to schedule in high pay off activities. If you can, consider blocking out a specific day(s) for your INFLUENCE activities. For instance, block out "writing days", if you are an aspiring author.

The monthly section is intended to help you project the milestones you intend to reach throughout the year. These milestones are targets to help you stay the course. This is a proactive design tool, intended to help you carve out the time and establish higher-level goals throughout the year. Keep it with you in a day timer and review it once a week.

The questions I've asked you along the right column are intended to help you focus your energy on what you want most, so please do your best in answering them as they will align your actions with your INFLUENCE in the world.

MY GET CLEAR PLAN

CLARITY | LEGACY | ENERGY | ATTITUDE | RECEIVING

My Prioritization Schedule at a Glance:

	MON	TUES	WED	THURS	FRI
EARLY RISER 6:00 – 8:00AM					
EARLY MORNING 8:00 – 10:00AM					
MID MORNING 10:00 – 12:00AM					
AFTERNOON 12:00 – 5:00PM					
EVENING EVENTS					

WHAT DO I WANT TO ACCOMPLISH MOST:

©COPYRIGHT REDCHAIR™ BRANDING INC.

My Monthly Milestones at a Glance:

JAN	FEB	MAR	APR	MAY	JUNE	JULY	AUG	SEPT	OCT	NOV	DEC

WHAT DO I WANT TO ACCOMPLISH MOST:

©COPYRIGHT REDCHAIR™ BRANDING INC.

Describe your success as if it has already occurred:

What do I want to create this Year?

My 5 BIGGEST goals are:

What do I want to be remembered for?

What brings me the most joy?

GERRY VISCA

Email Gerry Visca at gerry@redchairbranding.com to receive a PDF version of his GET CLEAR worksheet.

Affirmation

Work Sheet

Describe your future Influence in all areas of your life:

Career, Family, Love, Relationships and Finances.

Read out loud these "I AM" statements everyday.

I AM _____

_____

I AM _____

_____

I AM _____

_____

I AM _____

_____

I AM _____

_____

I AM _____

_____

I AM _____

_____

I AM _____

_____

Goal Setting

Work Sheet

List 3 life and leadership goals that will ignite your Influence.

1 _____

_____

2 _____

_____

3 _____

_____

List 3 NEXT-BEST actions you can take.

1 _____

_____

2 _____

_____

3 _____

_____

Scan this page to access this video training.

Personal Brand
Work Sheet

List 3 top attributes that best describes your influence. Focus on the core attributes that clearly differentiate you. <u>WHY</u> does it matter to others?

_____

_____

_____

_____

List the 3 images that best capture the essence of you:

_____

_____

_____

_____

Exercise your visual muscles.
Cut and paste images that best reflect
WHO you want to be and your Influence in the
world.

#1. This is my Influence

#1.

#2. This is who I want to be.

#2.

**#3. This is how
I want to be
remembered.**

#3.

Gerry Visca #whyguy
Inspirational Speaker | Author | Publisher

Gerry Visca is the WHY GUY on a mission to inspire 1 million Whys. His recent autobiographical, un-self-help books and transformational novel: Big Dreamers, I Don't Know What the Hell I'm Doing® and Remembering Why are helping people get clear on why they exist.

His education in architecture opened his mind to the world. He sharpened his skills as an award-winning Creative Director through him company, Redchair Branding. His global work as an inspirational speaker and creative coach inspires leaders and organizations to shift their energy and focus towards creating a new **ROI** for the world; one where we know why we exist and Reach Out and Inspire others.

His writing is expressed daily in his Why Blog, which he usually writes from his terrace, while enjoying a cup of freshly brewed coffee, sitting next to his love Angela. The transformational publications he creates, as the founder of Defyeneurs®, evolve out of a desire to inspire everyday people to do extraordinary things. He is honoured by his recent opportunity to have been published in Jack Canfield's latest book: *Living the Success Principles.*

Email gerry@redchairbranding.com

Face Book facebook.com/gerryvisca

Twitter @ Instagram @gerryvisca

Reach out to Gerry, if you wish...he's an open book!
www.gerryvisca.com www.defyeneurs.com

You can also book Gerry Visca as your inspirational speaker on WHY POWER through his International Speaking Bureau:
www.nsb.com
1.800.360.1073